Fearless Faith

PRISCILLA R. HALEY

Cocoon to Wings
PUBLISHING

Printed in the United States of America

ISBN: 978-1-64255-451-9

Published by Cocoon to Wings Publishing

Oviedo, Florida 32765

www.StephanieOutten.com

(813) 906-WING

The authors have tried to recreate events, locales and conversations from their memories of them. In order to maintain their anonymity in some instances, the names of individuals, places, identifying characteristics and details such as physical properties, occupations, and places of residence, may have been changed.

Unless otherwise noted, all scripture references are from the New King James Version and King James Version of the Holy Bible (Public Domain).

Cover design and Interior layout design by Ereka Thomas Designs

Fearless Faith

PRISCILLA R. HALEY

Contents

MORE BOOKS BY PRISCILLA R. HALEY

Broken but God

God Girlzs With A Vision

Gracefully Broken

Dedication

Life will often present new and exciting challenges, and yet it can also bring new fears, anxieties, and temptations. We worry about our children, our families, our jobs and our health. We stress over deadlines. We struggle with temptations and the pressures of LIFE.

We spend our days liking and posting on social media. *How many likes can I get? How many followers do I have?* We focus too much on the world's way, and we are afraid to share our faith with others.

The stories in *Fearless Faith* were written by women who've been tried by the fire and came out stronger and wiser. These are stories of women who know exactly what you're going through.

This book is dedicated to our sisters who feel their faith has failed them. Draw strength from God's Word as you read the encouragement and hope that's offered in the chapters of these brave women. Keep trusting in God and living your best life with *FEARLESS FAITH!*

Acknowledgments

First and foremost, I would like to thank God for the vision He gave to me for Fearless Faith, for trusting me and making the provisions to see it come to fruition. In the process of putting this book together, I realized how true the gift of writing is for me. You have given me the power to believe in my passion and pursue the calling you have on my life, to inspire and uplift my sisters. I could never have done this without the fearless faith I have in you, God Almighty.

To my mother, Virginia Louise Jefferson, who is no longer with us- I thank God for all of the prayers you prayed over me. You showed me how Faith the size of a mustard seed could move mountains. I wish you were here to see all of the giants slayed in my life because of my unwavering faith, that fearless faith in God that you instilled in me. To my father, Frank Jefferson, for the first time in 30 years I am speechless! I can barely find the words to express all the wisdom, love and support you've given me. You are my number one fan and for that I am eternally grateful. If I am blessed to live long enough, I hope I will be as good a prayer warrior to my kids and grandkids as you are, and always have been, to me. I Love You, Dad!

To my husband, Darin Haley - What can I say? You are one of the main reasons that my life has changed. I am so thankful that I have you in my corner pushing me when I am ready to give up. Thank you for having patience with me in taking on yet another challenge which cut into our date nights and fun trips. I promise I will make it up to you. You have stood beside me throughout this journey and writing this book. You have been my inspiration and motivation for continuing to improve my knowledge and move my career forward. You are my rock, and I am honored to call you my husband.

A big thanks to all my girlfriends and prayer warriors for sharing my happiness, always supporting me and giving me constructive feedback and encouragement. Never judging, but loving me unconditionally for who I am. When it seemed too difficult to keep going, you all prayed relentlessly and spoke life back into me. I would have probably given up on this book project without your support and unwavering faith.

Ereka Thomas of Ereka Thomas Designs – I extend heartfelt thanks from the bottom of my heart. I gave you my vision for the book cover, and you brought it to life. Words cannot express how much I appreciate you. Thank you! Thank you! Thank you!

Emily Claudette Freeman of E. Claudette Freeman Literary Services, you have done it again! You poured your heart and soul into Fearless Faith. You went above and beyond pulling at the heartstring of each one of the authors to make this book come to life. My editor for life! I love you, my sister!

Tracy L. Carter of Sista Girl Publications – Thank you for coming in at the ninth hour to proofread the chapters, and for helping us move this book project into its final stages. I cannot thank you enough!

Lastly, this book would not have been possible without my sister in Christ, Stephanie Outten of Cocoon to Wings Publishing. I am so grateful for the bond we have created. I didn't know, but God knew all along how He would bring us together. It was challenging at times, but you hung in there with me, giving it your all to make sure this work would not only represent us, but more than ever represent our Father in Heaven. Thank you for pouring into this book project. Thank you for the many conference calls and late nights reading and re-reading the ladies' stories to make sure our readers get the best and are able to resonate with each chapter. You are an amazing woman of God. I love you!

Living by Fearless Faith,

Priscilla R. Haley

Foreword

In reading and digesting the material in *Fearless Faith* I cannot help but wonder if the ten authors who collaborated to document their journeys in *Fearless Faith* are representative of the fearlessness of women's faith worldwide. What an extraordinarily powerful world we live in. I am honored to introduce you, the readers, to such an extraordinary compilation of faith activated.

My friend, Priscilla Haley , has a warm, compassionate, loving heart for God and His people. Her light shines best and brightest when she is serving and helping others become who God intended them to be, while living in divine purpose with passion.

Priscilla and I first met at a mutual friend's home, but really got to know each other better at another friend's home about a year or so later. We immediately recognized one another as being one of God's girls on a mission. That night at our friend's home, we had gut wrenching laughs, played games and had a wonderful time. Getting to know Priscilla has been an absolute joy. We knew we were destined to be a part of each other's lives from the start.

Priscilla knew she wanted to publish a book. Because she moves with intention, she did not rush in. Allowing the idea to marinate through prayer, fasting and meditation, she eventually knew what needed to be done; what she was being guided to do and what was required of her. She birthed *Fearless Faith*.

Fearless Faith is a book with an underlying message which teaches we are the righteousness of God in Christ Jesus and how we are to walk with the Lord in that righteousness. She wants people to know you can enjoy peace and joy in life by activating your faith. Galatians 5:6 says Faith works by love.

Along with clarity of the type of book she wanted to publish, a collaboration, came the names of the women who were to contribute to this Master's-piece. There was no need to advertise for contributors. She knew in her heart who the authors were to be.

Each of us have a story to tell, a story we have lived, and with some, are living. There may be a few of you who are in the midst of your story right now. You may not know how it will end. Well, that's exactly what this book addresses and stresses. If you are, or think you are, going through hell, don't stop! Keep moving. One foot in front of the other, you will get to the other side!

The contributing authors have elaborately weaved together a guideline for walking through the stressful times, whether it is an abusive relationship, divorce, sexual or physical abuse, losing everything from a natural disaster, addictions, financial strain, death or grief, even co-dependency. It does not matter what the situation is. There is hope. You, too, will come into the light once you activate your faith and develop an audacious, fearless faith in the One who can and will solve your problem.

Maybe you are not in a storm right now. That's great! I believe life is about ebb and flow. The tide comes in and retreats. That is kind of like how life is. We maneuver our way in and out of the many changes we face in life, some good, some challenging. We can still live with joy. It all comes down to faith and what we do with it.

The book, *Fearless Faith*, is here to challenge your thinking, challenge you to stretch your faith like never before, set afire passions, and bring to life those dreams you set aside, to challenge you to live life to the full by letting go of what no longer serves you and developing a deeper faith you never thought you could have. You can have that deep faith and more! Fearless Faith will let you see how ten other power-filled women set their lives ablaze. Faith is the gift that keeps on giving and grows when nurtured and exercised. These women show how they were able to walk through the darkest times of their lives straight into the light and live a life of fullness. They may have been battered and bruised, but they are the better for all they have gone through.

Can you imagine living the life you have always wanted to live but there was something blocking that from happening? You still can.

Fearless Faith speaks on tragedy to triumph, but it is much more than that, by far. It is life changing. Through these women's stories, they have bared every tear ever formed was running down my cheeks. Pain, fear, frustration, hate, anger… it was all flowing onto my floor. I curled up into a ball with my little white Shih Tzu, Runt, licking my face, and I cried. I think I called my dad, and my mom came over. She got on the floor with me and held my head in her lap. She stroked my hair and told me that whatever it was, it was going to be all right. Once again God sent me a lifeline. My mom picked me up off the floor, gathered me up in her arms and took Runt and me to her and my dad's house. I found atmospheric peace within the four walls of my room at their house, but my soul was still at war. It was this breakdown that sent my parents looking for help. They found an inpatient treatment facility and my mom took me. I remember the conversation and visit between me, my mom, and the doctor like it was yesterday:

"Maybe we should check her in? Three-day treatment in house," said this petite lady with wavy hair. I assumed she was the doctor.

I looked at her, "NO! NO! NO!" I said, but she just kept talking to my mom. Maybe she didn't hear me? So, I got louder, "No! I can't lose my job. They are going to think I'm crazy. Not fit for duty."

While my mom and the doctor continued to talk I remember thinking to myself; *How did I end up here? How did I – Crisis Intervention Team trained officer, get here? In this state of mind?* It was like a huge tug of war between normal and abnormal, and abnormal was winning! I was stuck in the middle. If anyone found out I was here I could just imagine what they would say. They already talk about me. *Slut. Home wrecker. Drama filled. Trouble.* I guess they can just add crazy to the list as well. But I can't be labeled again. Once you're labeled in this job, in this department, it will never go away. I already have enough labels. Between tears I pleaded to go home, "I will lose my job if you keep me here. I worked so hard for it. My house. My dog. Who will take care of my dog? Please ma'am, please." We agreed to outpatient treatment starting with once a week visits. And with that compromise, I was on my way home.

My first session with Saudia, I remember us just looking at each other. I didn't want to talk, and she didn't push. My sessions started out once a week their souls for you to apply to your life the steps they took, the encouraging words, Bible scriptures and prayers they offer.

Your brighter day is waiting on you. Blessings to you on your path to Fearless Faith. You have come this far by faith, now is the time to go even further.

Marsha Sherrill

Victorious God's girl,
Author, Speaker, Mentor

"In the multitude of my anxieties within me, Your comforts delight my soul." Psalm 94:19

CHAPTER I

MONICA L. FORTSON

Bruised But Not Broken

"And we know that in all things God works for the good of those who love Him, who have been called according to His purpose."

Romans 8:28

When my aunt first asked me to write a chapter for her book I was excited to share with the world about what God had brought me through. I mean, I had already shared through ministry many of the things I planned on writing about. But, as the deadline got closer I found myself finding more and more reasons not to write my testimony. The devil began to put fear into my mind that I wouldn't touch lives. That my testimony held no value. He began to whisper in my ear that being transparent and open about the experiences of my life would bring about gossip. That my job would be in jeopardy. That I would be talked about and laughed at. I began to feel anxiety about my testimony. I began to question whether this project was for me.

I sat down and started to research scriptures for my chapter. During my search, God gave me Romans 8:28 (NIV), "And we know that in all things God works for the good of those who love Him, who have been called according to His purpose." Though my life cannot fit into five thousand words,

I pray the portion that I share touches your heart. I pray that it brings healing and understanding to some part of your own journey. I pray that at the end of these five thousand words you know that you are not alone. And that someone else has already – or is currently - walking the crumbled path with you. I pray that as you read my journey to finding my fearless faith you see that through the transparency of sharing my experiences and my testimony, I am unmasking myself. I have traveled outside of the will of God but have always found my way back home in the end. I am not selling you a story. I am telling you my life.

❧——☙

"But he refused to listen to her, and since he was stronger than she, he raped her."

2 Samuel 13:14 NIV

I can never get back what they took from me that night. They took my happiness, my security, my joy, my love. They took my womanhood, that night. That night, they took my self-esteem. They took my trust in people. They took me. Each one of them took a little bit of me with them that night.

Who is this girl I look at in the mirror? She has so much unspoken pain and anger behind her smile. So much self-hatred behind her laugh. This girl I'm looking at looks exactly like me, but different. She is now different inside. She still secretly cries herself to sleep at night, wanting no one and everyone to embrace her. After all this time, nobody knows the secret she carries because of that night.

That night changed everything. How can they have families? How can they get married? Why do all my relationships fall apart? But theirs… theirs seem perfect.

How many have I given myself to after that night? I lost count a long time ago. I did everything to get those parts of me back that they took that night. Yet, I kept losing more parts of me. Who is there to care? That night they took without permission, so I gave without care. Without emotion. Without a second thought.

Working as a sexual assault investigator and teaching sexual assault investigation techniques to colleagues, I learned (and teach) that the act of sexual assault is about power for the attacker. It's about control, not necessarily pleasure. I share that more than half of sexual assault survivors freeze during the assault. They experience Rape Induced Paralysis. Most survivors know their attacker. This was all true for me.

I was sitting in sexual assault training at Texas Southern University in 2014 when the speaker played a recording of a drunk female calling 911 to report she had been raped by a friend. She was crying, self-blaming, and slurring her speech. We listened to her try and understand why he chose her. And then it happened. I began to cry. I began to feel sick to my stomach. I could feel the vomit stirring in my stomach. I could smell the cranberry and vodka shots I had thrown back that night. I saw myself stumbling around the parking lot, riding in the truck and throwing up on the side of my bed. I could hear his voice saying to the others, "No. Let's go!" In the middle of the conference room, I felt myself, again, rolling over onto my back, and the pressure against my shoulders. And then, nothing. I was experiencing my first trigger. I got up and walked outside the conference room. I needed air. I needed to get away from everyone. I needed to forget again.

Years prior to this first trigger, my mom called me. She and my dad were still living in Seattle, and my brother and I had been in Houston since 2005. We chit chatted for a minute or so, but I knew there was something else.

"Is there a video of you passed out with multiple guys having sex with you?" She asked. I could hear in her voice that she was scared and concerned.

I laughed, "No mom. Where did you hear that from?" My gut was uneasy. I had truly blocked out my rape. After I gave her the answer I believed she was hoping for, we said our goodbyes and hung up. From that day forward, I tried functioning like nothing had happened to me. But, that night had taken hold of my life and every part of who I was without me even knowing it. Without me being able to control it. That night had taken over my mind, heart and relationships. It had taken over how I valued and viewed myself. I was living under the control of that night.

I have never had a problem getting a man. But, I have always had problems keeping one! I remember joking one time with my older cousin about having a "keep a man problem." A huge part of this, I understand now, was that night kept setting up shop in every relationship I would have. Whether it was an intimate platonic relationship or a romantic one. My trust in people was no longer there and I had a wall around my heart with no entryway.

In the years following my rape I found myself jumping from one relationship to the next. Falling in love and falling right back out. Moving from one bed to the next and back to mine. Searching for that "something." Never really stopping to figure out what that something really was. Dating men that reflected how I felt about myself, broken and damaged. Secretly wishing the next one would be my savior and magically make this pain go away. Hoping that the next one would bring me peace within my heart and mind (it was a daily battle going on in both). And all the time, I was putting on for the people that I was intelligent, confident, secure in who I was, unbothered by my constant change in partners and that I had it all together. Each morning I would wake up and make up the outside, subconsciously saying to myself that if the outside looked good the inside wouldn't matter. But, the inside did matter. Because the inside was carrying a pain so deep not a single pill I would swallow could take it away.

⚬——⚬

"Pray without ceasing; in everything give thanks; for this is the will of God in Christ Jesus for you."

1 Thessalonians 5:17-18 NKJV

In 2011, I found myself in a deep depression. I was self-medicating through unhealthy relationships. I was growing angrier; and was no fun to be around. But, still couldn't figure out why. At the end of 2012, I had a break up with a longtime friend and that's when I remember everything starting to unravel. After I got back from visiting him in California he ended our short-lived relationship. I remember lying on my couch and crying. And when I was all cried out I just continued to lie there. I couldn't move. I was so tired. Tired of life. Tired of relationships. Tired of being tired. I'm not even sure how long I lay there, but I know it was for a while. I began to contemplate suicide… then my phone rang.

"Hey buddy!" It was my childhood friend, Tre. Man, God knows when to send a lifeline! This was my phone-a-friend (the term "phone-a-friend" came from the game show where you have life lines and one of them is to phone a friend). God said suicide was not my final answer. It was a brief reprieve; a few months later I was self-medicating again with the most amazing man ever, until he wasn't. We were sitting in his bed one morning and his cell phone rang. He didn't answer it. No big deal.

Then the house phone rang. I didn't even know he had one! The answering machine kicked on and her voice filled the room. "I know you're in there! I see her car parked in the driveway. Answer the door." Then the doorbell rang. I looked at him, and he got out the bed and told me to stay in the room. There was an exchange at the door, and then she appeared in the doorway of the bedroom. I don't remember what she said to me, but she was polite. She turned and walked back outside. When he came back inside I lost it! I started to connect the dots. *"That's whose hairbrush was in the drawer,"* I thought to myself. That relationship ended. And the next one began.

I'm not sure after which break up it happened. But, I once again found myself laid out on my couch. This time it was for days. My parents would come over and I would just lie there. They would talk to me and I would lie there. They would get mad and I would still just lie there. I couldn't get up. My body wouldn't allow me to get up. My mind wouldn't allow me to get up. It wouldn't allow me to do anything but lie there. I had no energy. No desire to live. Nothing. I was tired. Tired of life. Tired of the constant let downs. Tired of the heartbreak. I was done. At some point, I finally made my way to my bedroom floor and broke down crying. Uncontrollable crying. It was like then moved to twice a month. They moved to once a month and now we meet whenever I want/need to talk. Being diagnosed with anything sucks. But, being diagnosed with some type of mental illness double sucks. It's embarrassing. Shameful. It's like that ugly scar you don't want to show when you're dressed up real nice for a night out. Or that one thing that nobody in the family wants to talk about. You know *that* thing. Whatever reason God saw fit to give major depression to me, I didn't understand at the time nor did I care. I just wanted to be normal. But, like Saudia would always ask me, "What is normal?"

Everyone has something. My "something" was depression. There have been times when battling my mood swings, tiredness, lack of appetite, over-eating, binge eating, anti-socialness, and whatever else comes along with depression, has had me wanting to give up. It seemed like the more progress I made with Saudia understanding my illness, the worse it got. I would get to a place of self-love and feeling like I didn't need counseling or medication. I would be on the up and then, BAM! A man would come to take me off track. And the cycle happened all over again. Girl meets boy. Girl opens her heart to boy. Boy breaks girl's heart. Girl ends up on the couch of her therapist again. Throughout the years of my talks with Saudia, she has, and still to this day, told me that I have got to get to a place where Monica is happy with just Monica - happiness that is not dictated by something or someone.

There aren't very many people that know I have a counselor or that I have a diagnosis of major depression (well I guess there is now). I felt like it was something I had to hide from everyone outside of a couple of boyfriends, friends, and a few family members. The first time I really shared to the masses was when I was asked to speak at Brentwood Baptist Church during their youth service. I really didn't know what I was going to say. The morning of, still having not the slightest idea, I got up and once again God directed me to what He wanted and needed me to say. I grabbed my backpack, loaded it up with bricks, my make-up bag, gun belt, and uniform shirt. Then headed out the house. I arrived early, greeted everyone, and grabbed some coffee. As the service started, the kids were dancing to music and inquiring about who I was. I showed them a dance I learned as a youth counselor at a church camp when I volunteered for Bethel's Family Church. Then, it was time. I walked on stage and began to tell them about my best friend. How we grew up close with each other and were inseparable. How through high school we were thick as thieves but entering college we lost contact with each other. I told the kids that a year or so ago we found each other again, and while we were catching up and learning where the other one had been, she told me her story.

I told them how she entered college and ended up in a relationship that started off amazing. They were in love. Lived together and everything. But about a year into the relationship he began to change. He became verbally abusive and she gave it right back to him. They would yell and curse at each other and then make up. In one of the arguments he grabbed her and threw her into the front door of his apartment, she blacked out for a second and he kicked her in her back. She wanted to end the relationship, but love kept her there. She told herself if she changed or if she did whatever he wanted, he would go back to how, and who, he was when they very first started dating. But, he didn't. He continued to lie, cheat, and abuse her.

I reached into my makeup bag and grabbed some lipstick. While putting it on I told them how my friend would wake up in the morning and make up her face and smile all day as she walked around campus. Nobody knew the burden she carried. I told them that once my friend's parents found out what had happened, they moved her out of state and she started her senior year of college in a fresh new Christian environment. Though her environment and location were new, the pain she brought with her was old. She was broken and longed to have a good healthy relationship, so she started dating. Picking men that told her how beautiful she was. How amazing her body was and how they loved her. She overlooked the late-night phone calls. The women whispering to each other when she and her man were out. The rumors of other women being pregnant by her man. She overlooked all of that because she was not going to have another relationship end like the one back home.

I told them about the time my friend was out drinking one night, and she ended up being raped. I told them how she never told anyone. I closed by telling them that my friend eventually graduated from college. Did some teaching for a few years and, as I put on my gun belt, became a Houston Police Officer. I told them that friend I found a year or so ago was standing in front of them now. She was ME! The look on their faces was pure shock! I went on to close by walking down the aisle taking out each brick I still carried in my backpack and dropping it on the floor. Telling them how you never know what a person is going through or carrying just by looking at them. You never know what the inside of someone looks like. After service, one of the girls told me that I didn't look like what I had been through. And to this day that is the best and most thoughtful compliment I have ever received. This was the start of my journey to fearless faith.

❧——❧

"In those days that you pray, I will listen."

Jeremiah 29:12 NKJV

The Aftermath: the period immediately following a usually ruinous event; the period after a bad and usually destructive event. Aftermath.

The storm came without warning. You didn't see it coming. It tore through your life, faith, security, hope, dreams, heart, stability, and love. You held on during the storm to anything that could keep you grounded, but you were still tossed around, beaten up, bruised, and broken. Now the aftermath feels worse than the storm. You are left to pick up the pieces from a storm that has no idea what it left in its wake. It came through and did what it was created to do - destroy and move on.

But the aftermath... the period AFTER the storm. The period of rebuilding, reliving, creating new... the period of reconstruction. This period is left to you.

I am living in my aftermath. The period after my storm. There have been many storms and many reconstruction periods. I am sure there will be more to come, but this time it is different. I will be completely honest with you. I don't have a step by step to tell you how to get to your place of healing. You just do. What I can tell you, though, is that it has been a process. A journey. I have been a process and journey within myself. And I am still a work in progress. I recognize that I have scars from my many battles, but the pain is no longer there. They may get sore from time to time and that's okay. But these scars are healed. No longer to be opened. And that is by choice.

In the journey to loving myself I discovered that many of the feelings we feel are by choice. We can choose to stay mad at someone or something. We can choose to forgive or allow our emotions to be overrun with things and people we cannot change. We can choose to live hostage to the things the devil tries to bury us in, or we can choose to give it to God. At some point, I chose to give it to God. I don't have an exact date when I gave it all to HIM. Or an amazing come-to-Jesus moment where I knew HE was in full control. Nope. That's not my life. What I do have, though, is HIS promise, "In those days when you pray, I will listen (NKJV)." I have had many days where I wasn't sure, because of the way I was living my life, if my Father would recognize my voice if I spoke out to Him. But, just like a parent can be in the middle of a crowded mall and recognize their child's cry yards away, our Father will never forget our voice. I had many days where I felt as though I was too far gone for Him to reach me and pull me back in. But, in Thessalonians 5:17, He says, "never stop praying." My mom and dad would tell me and my brother growing up, "There is nothing you could ever do so bad that I would stop loving you." Jesus is the same. He created each one of us, unique and special in our own right. He created us knowing every tear, smile, laugh, heartbreak, win, and loss we would ever experience.

Learning how to love yourself is hard and can be painful; but, it's worth the journey. As I have come to find my fearless faith in myself I learned to recognize my weaknesses. My desire to be a wife and a mother led me to chase and live within unhappy, unhealthy, and unnecessary relationships. I put myself on a timeline based upon my friends and other women my age as to when I needed to be married with kids. This self-imposed timeline convinced me to put myself on sale on more than one occasion. But you know what? The sale has ended!

Too many of us ladies, me included, have placed our hearts, bodies, souls, and very essence of who we are, "on sale." We have marked down our price so those who normally could not afford us could purchase us at half our value. And once they have purchased us for less than, they treat us as though the price we allowed them to purchase us for is truly our real worth. Our original price had many window shoppers but no buyers. So, thinking that our price was too expensive we put ourselves on sale. Not realizing we were priced at our correct value and it was the people shopping that needed to upgrade.

See, those window shoppers that couldn't afford the original price: you know the ones that came and looked, tried on but didn't buy, were never meant to own such a high-quality item! If we are honest with ourselves and honest with our God, we must admit that there were signs he was not the one. Because we live in a "I–need-it–to-happen-now. I can't let her get a man before me. I'm not complete without a man on my arm," mentality; we tricked ourselves into believing our God-given sticker price was incorrect and we needed to take it upon ourselves to adjust and lower our price so more people could afford us. My loves, cheaper does not always mean better. Just because more people can afford us doesn't mean we are now priced correctly.

The thing about a high sticker price is that it tells people I am not cheap. I am not for everyone. You must work hard to afford me and if you are blessed to be able to purchase such a high -quality item such as myself, my value will never diminish. Like a fine wine the more time that goes by the better I get.

Though I am still not a mother, I do have kids. Throughout this entire journey God was giving me everything I desired. He opened my heart to youth and youth ministry. He gave me access to youth programs through my job; where I continue to keep in contact with some of the kids. He has given me access to share my life with young boys and girls in jail. He placed me in the position to be a mother figure to those kids that had not experienced that love or just needed extra compassion. He has given me a small army of beautiful God children that love me for who I am and vice versa. He allowed me to walk through and survive these stormy relationships to have a better appreciation for the husband He will send me when the time is right. He has carried me to and through some stuff. Pushed me through some stuff. And walked with me through some stuff. He has never given up on me. Even when I had given up on myself. I lost some things when I held on so tight to people that He was trying to remove from my life. The things that I lost are beginning to come back.

In December 2015, I was at Lakewood Church, Houston, Texas, to hear Pastor John Gray. In his sermon, "The Crossover," he said, "God allows things to happen to show you there are some holes in your foundation… HE is filling up holes so when you occupy the thing you are created for, you are prepared." In the same sermon he stated, "Your storm is proportionate to your destination." I truly believe these two things.

Being called to ministry is an amazing calling. Most of us think that it is limited to preaching and pastoring. Being called to minister can be God whispering to you to say a prayer for someone. It may be giving a simple smile at the lady walking past you; or giving the homeless man on the corner your homemade lunch (yes, the one you wanted all night and excitedly packed in your lunch bag). Ministering to someone else brings about a feeling of compassion for the next person. Your small prayer may be the lifeline they needed. But, don't forget to minister to yourself.

When things were going great in my life it was very easy for me to praise Him and thank Him for all that I had and what was happening in my life. When things were at rock bottom it was very easy for me to call out to Him and beg for Him to take this pain away and change my situation. But, when I was in the middle I fell away from prayer and communication with the Father. My Father. When things were going okay, I could maintain from day to day. And when things were bad, but I had experienced worse, I could maintain from day to day. As I write and look back I can't help but wonder to myself what if I would have prayed.

Prayer and a constant communication with God will change your circumstances and life. It may not happen when, where, and how we want, but it will happen. Being in fellowship with a church can keep you grounded and connected to the body of worship if you allow it. I know we can struggle with church sometimes. I have… especially when I've worked an overnight shift or worked six days straight and this Sunday is the only day I will have off for another six days, but still go. Go and allow your heart to be opened, healed or mended. Go and allow the congregation to love on you. Allow the usher to give you that handshake and hug as they greet you walking in. Go and allow your feet to carry you to the altar to be prayed over. Go and allow someone to stand with you and in the gap for you. Just go. (Note to self: adhere to what you're writing!)

I have and have had many friends that the experience of church is just not for them. They don't have the right clothes. Or they've had the leader of the new membership committee frown upon them because they had a child out of wedlock. Put those things aside and worship. If that church is snooty, (yes there are some like that), find another one. We, as Christians, cannot forget the journey we took to get to where we are in our faith. When we forget or hide our own past we have the potential to do real damage to those that want to love the Lord just as much as we do, but don't know where to start. When my aunt asked me to write, she did so by sending me a post I had written on Facebook a while back so, as I wrap up this peek into my life I'll leave you with this; God didn't ask for your opinion or approval, He just asked you to love.

As you move forward in your own journey in finding your fearless faith, remember there is someone out there who has or is going through a season of storms. You are not alone, and you will never be alone if you allow God to be in the driver's seat of your life.

Building Your Fearless Faith Muscle:

1. Pray

2. Be patient in the process

3. When you fall; pick yourself back up and keep moving forward

4. Let go and let God

5. Know and believe that with each battle you face, you will survive

CHAPTER 2
TATAYANDA JOHNSON-YOUNGER

Transparently Transitioning My Fears into Fearless Faith

"Now may the God of hope fill you with all joy and peace in believing, that you may abound in hope by the power of the Holy Spirit."

Romans 15:13

Can you imagine a month before your wedding date finding out that your soon-to-be husband has been cheating on you? No one should ever have to experience that type of emotional trauma…the type of trauma I had to endure. God's grace has carried me through some turbulent trials, and it was no different when I found out my then-fiancé, Brian, was unfaithful. The encounters were taking place with a woman named Tina, whom he supposedly knew from church. I had some suspicions that something peculiar was transpiring, but I lacked enough evidence to consider my intuition as factual.

One afternoon, Brian abruptly told me that he was going on a business trip. Normally he would inform me of his schedule weeks in advance. His phone activity had become noticeably strange – suddenly he was getting an unusual amount of text messages at night and during the early morning hours.

Any time that I asked Brian anything about his increased phone activity, a heated argument would spark. His mannerisms made me feel like he was distancing himself from me – the affection wasn't as loving and playful as it had been. I attempted to refrain from leaning on my own ideas about what was going on. Through prayer, I would ask God to reveal if my discernment was accurate, or if Satan was attempting to steal my peace of mind about my relationship with Brian.

On several occasions, I asked Brian if he had a social media page. He told me, "No." I was not into social media during that phase of my life. However, I searched his name on the Internet and several self-incriminating pictures appeared on the computer screen. I was heartbroken but had some semblance of peace that my thoughts had been confirmed.

When I approached Brian with my questions and concerns, he was very nonchalant and arrogant. I was told that nothing had happened, and that Tina was just a friend from church. The pictures were taken in a hotel room and the dates on the photos coincided with days that Brian told me he was going out of town with his job. What made matters even more painful was the fact that I had recently given birth to our first beautiful daughter, India. I was at home with her alone and battling with postpartum depression while he was out cheating. That day, I lost most of my trust in Brian, and for me things would never quite be the same between us. I shared my anguish with him. I cried. He cried. We were both in a painful place not quite sure how we would make it out. He apologized and promised he would spend the rest of his life fixing his wrong doings and regaining my trust. Did I fully believe him? At the time, I couldn't say for sure. But fear crept into the crevices of my heart, and I knew then that I would have to lean and depend on God for restoration, comfort and guidance. Most of all, I needed an increase in my faith to believe in him again.

It was a combination of Brian's remorse and Christian pre-marital counseling that gave me a sense of hope that we could still have a successful union in spite of his infidelity. The Minister and Counselor, Reverend Paul Carpenter, advised us that we did not need to get married if the trust between us wasn't restored. He spoke of the importance of forgiveness as he was preparing to join us together in marriage. I had been in constant communication with God through prayer while working on forgiving Brian. A part of me believed that we would be all right. In addition, most of our invited guests had begun reserving their spot for the ceremony and I had just submitted the final payment to the event planner. Honestly, I felt compelled to go ahead and get married instead of letting everyone down – even if it meant letting myself down. Although I still did not trust Brian, I desired so deeply to trust him again. Exercising faith in God was vital as I leaned on Him in order to remedy the negative impact Brian's cheating had on my heart. I trusted that our situation would get better.

Our wedding day finally arrived. We had a beautiful ceremony and a great turnout. I was feeling optimistic about our future together. My focus was on moving forward with Brian as a married couple, while leaving our past behind us. Reverend Paul Carpenter conducted our wedding and prayed over us multiple times as we stood at the front of the room underneath a bright spotlight. Brian and I exchanged vows and made a commitment before God to love and honor each other. We were united as one body in Christ.

Shortly after our union, Brian's family officially welcomed me. We attended multiple family gatherings and frequent dinner events together. I attempted to form a relationship with Brian's sister, Ellen. Our communication was a little odd at times. Ellen expressed to me that she did not accept me because I was taking away her only brother. Ellen influenced the majority of their family to dislike me. It was extremely apparent in the ways that they would treat me when I would come around them. Uncomfortable is how I felt the majority of the times. She made herself look like the victim when she was - in fact - the aggressor. Contrarily, Brian was on Ellen's side and very rarely spoke up for me pertaining to how his side of the family would treat me. I could not help but to view Brian differently because he would not put his sister in her place whenever she was out of line. This created negativity in our marriage. I realized I could not depend on Brian to defend me as his wife. I remained prayerful and placed my trust in God to strengthen our bond.

Over the course of ten years, Brian's infidelity increased. He felt his actions were justified according to his perceptions of right versus wrong. He would tell me that he was cheating because he was upset with me or because we had a disagreement. Brian consistently told me he was working twelve-hour shifts all seven days of the week. Sometimes that information was accurate, and other times it provided Brian with an opportunity to step out. Brian refused to allow me to touch his cell phone, which had a passcode. He took multiple precautions to ensure that I could not access or retrieve any additional information about his behaviors. It was a common practice for Brian to walk around our home with his phone on his hip with a blue tooth in his ear. While sleeping, Brian would place his phone underneath his pillow. His actions caused me to become insecure and anxious. I felt alone, overwhelmed, unloved and like a complete failure. We seldom had quality family time and date nights were obsolete. I longed for the little things that married couples did together such as traveling, grocery shopping and going on dates. My heart desired so deeply to trust him. But, Brian gave me every reason not to.

A little over a month after I became pregnant with our amazing son Jacob, I received a phone call from Brian while I was at work. He was crying hysterically. He had been diagnosed with a STD. The disease was a result of a sexual encounter he had with a woman he knew from college. My heart began beating rapidly, and all I could focus on at that moment was my health and the health of our unborn baby boy. Because of God's grace and mercy, my health and the baby's health were not compromised.

I cried uncontrollably as I gave God total praise for His goodness. I realized that I had spent the duration of my marriage trying to convince myself that my situation was not as toxic as it seemed. Making up excuses to justify the disrespect, dishonesty and disloyalty. The truth was our marriage was not based on Christian principles. Every aspect of our union was unhealthy, and it was not okay. I was fed up and done!

Although the two of us were withdrawn in every way imaginable, we continued to live together for the sake of our children. Still married under God's law, my husband and I became roommates. My stomach would churn, and I could feel bile rise up in my throat if Brian even tried to touch me. The pain was so severe I felt my heart being wretched from my chest when I looked at him. I didn't want to have anything to do with him. The thought of my babies becoming products of a broken home worried me. Neither Brian nor I were from a broken home. The possibilities of that scenario played back and forth in my mind daily until one Sunday morning God spoke to me through a sermon at Community Baptist Church. Pastor Winn Truman preached about being equally yoked in a marriage. During the sermon, he passionately released these words, "It is better for children to come from a broken home than for them to live in one!" Peter 5:7 (NKJV) states: "Casting all your care upon him, for he cares for you." I knew God had designed that word specifically for me that day. I could feel myself inching away from fear and closer to faith. Baby steps. One foot in front of the other, but like a baby hesitant to take the next step, I still stumbled. It's crazy what fear will do to you, right?

Our marriage was moving into another separation. We parted ways the first time when India was three years old. Brian moved out of our home for six months, and we only communicated about topics related to India, during that time. Now with two children, I was fearful – scared out of my mind. The road ahead of me appeared blocked by my inability to see past the dark storm clouds in my life. Nothing was working in our favor. Conversations about restoring and saving our marriage became futile. He was disinterested. I was uncomfortable. Long before we reached this breaking point, Brian had become comfortable with me being uncomfortable with the situations taking place. I let him know that it hurt me when he would keep secrets from me and refuse to be transparent in our marriage. He spent so much time away from us. I felt like I was a married single mother. It seemed like the more vocal I became; the less willing Brian was to make amends. I needed guidance and a piece of mind. I was tired of pulling my hair out every night. Unfocused thoughts consumed me. I knew it was time for me to prepare for an intense prayer therapy session with God. I looked to Him for strength. My God came through and carried me through my disoriented chaos.

I was a great, loving, faithful and supportive wife to Brian for a solid seven years. After being mistreated, ignored and taken for granted for so long, I began to shut down. As a defense mechanism, I went into a deep state of depression. I had no clue how to reverse the effects of the damage. I unintentionally removed myself from being in contact with my close family members and friends. I found myself consuming alcohol more often than normal as a temporary means to bypass the turmoil that I was facing. The alcohol became my safe haven, my refuge – even if only for a little while. The warning signs were directly in my view, but I ignored them and pretended that they did not exist. I no longer wanted to be submissive and found it utterly difficult to engage in sexual intercourse with Brian because I resented him. I was disgusted with the way Brian treated me. I released myself from worrying about how our family, friends and other people would feel about our circumstances. The Lord emphasized to me the importance of being obedient to Him. At that point, I began placing all of my focus and attention on God. All I wanted to do was to get out and break free! I refused to be unhappy and miserable for the remainder of my life. Deep inside I knew that God *had to have* something better in store for me.

After constantly praying and crying, I finally mustered up the strength to file for divorce. What I prayed would be a short process turned into a six-month long, drawn out process. Brian was being obstructive and would not sign the paperwork. I was afraid and unsure about what was getting ready to happen. Through it all, I remained strong in my belief that God was going to step in and intervene. Although the journey ahead of me was not going to be easy, the good Lord was going to make a way. I faced my fears with courage and I demanded and commanded those mountains to move! Depression, lack of confidence, anxiety, fear, worry, and unnecessary stress, no longer had a place in my life, in the name of Jesus! I worshipped God through my pain and despair. The fear that I had been facing began to miraculously transform into fearless faith.

During my transitional process, I found myself heading down a new path of destruction. My friend, Sasha, introduced me to an older man named

Mack. She and her husband Joseph spoke favorably of him. It was effortless for me to view Mack through a positive lens. As I attentively listened to all his great attributes, I became convinced that meeting Mack was exactly what I needed. I agreed to allow Sasha to give Mack my phone number.

A few days later, while I was at work, I received a text message from Mack. A vibrant smile formed on my face as I read the text, *"I was thinking about you and I hope that today is the best day of your life!"*

"Wow!" I loudly blurted out. That sign of hope from Mack intrigued me. Mack briefly introduced himself to me. He also included other information in the text that led me to believe that he was a man of God. I was listening and looking for hope in my dark place.

Mack and I had an incredible and innocent first date. Coupled with our prior conversations, we became immediately attracted and drawn to each other like magnets. As time progressed, our communication increased by phone, text messages and in person. We saw each other every day. I admired the fact that chronologically he was seventeen years older than I was. In my vulnerable mind, an older man meant a wiser man. Mack wined and dined me and said the right things. Often, he would confidently boast to me that he was "The Catch." Early each morning we would talk on the phone and pray together before we went to work. That was a practice that I was not accustomed to in a relationship. From my interpretation, Mack was my special angel sent from God. He made me feel so important, beautiful, desired and happy. I was overfilled with intense joy when I would see or hear from Mack.

Mack would often look me in my eyes and tell me he had fallen in love with me, and on several occasions asked me to be his wife. We were both dealing with drastic life changing events, which seemed to have left us semi-paralyzed emotionally, so healing needed to take place before marriage was an option. Brian and I was going through a divorce, and Mack had lost his second wife due to a battle against an aggressive form of cancer, less than two years before we met each other. My two precious children, India and Jacob, adored the times we would spend together with Mack and his wonderful two sons. Our enjoyable journey together suddenly began to disintegrate after

Mack and I found out that I was pregnant. From that moment, his sweet thoughtful words and gestures began to disappear. Mack started distancing himself from me and became less available during the times I needed him the most. Many days and nights, I would cry myself to sleep while attempting to fully understand exactly why I was going through yet another turbulent storm in my life.

I began to question and doubt myself all at the same moment. *What is it that you want me to do next?* I asked God with tears racing down my face. The gentle voice of my Lord and Savior Jesus Christ whispered in my ear and said, "Child of mine, I've got you and you are going to be just fine!" I was reminded of I Corinthians 10:13 (NKJV) which clearly states: "No temptation has overtaken you except such as is common to man; but God is faithful, who will not allow you to be tempted beyond what you are able, but with the temptation will also make the way of escape, that you may be able to bear it." The Lord our God will not put more on us than what we can handle. He allowed me to be faced with this situation as a result of my decision-making. My heart was crushed, and I felt helpless. I had no other choice but to surrender to God and to trust and believe in Him. I forgave myself, and I asked God for His forgiveness. My heart was humbled, and my direct healing process began to transpire and unfold.

Mack repeatedly requested that I abort our unborn baby or give her up for adoption directly after birth. How could he think that another woman could be a better mother to our child? I am a great mother and nurturer to my babies. Mack even went as far as having me watch abortion videos at his house, hoping to convince me that the procedure was not as gruesome and horrendous as it appeared to be. Boldly, I looked Mack in his eyes and told him, "I refuse to choose any of your insensitive options. I love God, you and myself too much to kill or get rid of our baby." If it were not meant for me to get pregnant by Mack, then the good Lord would not have allowed it to happen.

I was going to have to raise this baby – along with India and Jacob - alone. Mack made it clear that he did not want any more children - after he got me pregnant. His number one excuse - finances. The days turned into weeks and the weeks into months. Before long, my pregnant belly began to show. I told Mack that I had a sincere desire to meet his three adult daughters before my pregnancy progressed any further. He wasn't ready to inform his family that he had a baby on the way. He was embarrassed and worried about how he would be viewed by his family and friends. I was completely insulted by Mack's immature responses. I couldn't fathom a man *that old* being worried about what someone else would have to say about him and us, as if their lives were perfect and free of sins. Romans 3:23 (NKJV) states, "For all have sinned and fallen short of the glory of God."

There was a chapter in my life where I used to worry about how other people perceived me. The stress caused me to gain excessive weight. I was easily irritated, and I began to lose my focus on God and His divine purpose for my life. I found myself forced to prove to others that I was good enough. I faced moments where I had to demonstrate my worth for a job, in a relationship and in my failed marriage. Although people often neglected to see my value, God saw, and still sees the best in me and in all of us. It is not that I am not good enough. Because that is based off someone else's biased opinions of me. The truth is that I am good enough. In fact, I supersede all qualifications and expectations required to succeed. I am good enough just the way God created me! Engaging in purposeful prayer allowed me to change my mindset and provided me with sustainable peace and confidence that I was lacking. Purposeful prayer involves adding purpose and intent into your prayer life. It includes being specific about the desires of your heart. Purposeful prayer connects a believer of faith with God on a more intimate and spiritual level.

My delivery date was rapidly approaching. I asked Mack if he could be present at the hospital for the birth of our sweet baby girl, Miracle. He told me he wouldn't be there and that he was going out of town. Once again, I was left to face another challenging obstacle where I had to exercise my faith in God. I felt severely discouraged and afraid. I picked up my Bible and turned to Psalm 23 (NKJV), which reads, "The Lord is my Shepherd I shall not want. He makes me to lie down in green pastures; He leads me beside the still waters. He restores my soul; He leads me in the paths of righteousness for his name's sake. Yea, though I walk through the valley of the shadow of death, I will fear no evil; for you are with me; your rod and your staff, they comfort me. You prepare a table before me in the presence of my enemies; you anoint my head with oil; my cup runs over. Surely goodness and mercy shall follow me all the days of my life; And I will dwell in the house of the Lord Forever."

Instantly, I was reassured that I would not be left alone in a lonely, cold hospital, giving birth to my baby. God will never leave us or forsake us. My dependable, loving momma was there supporting me. She never left my side. I realize daily that I am blessed and have so many reasons to exhibit a grateful heart. While going through labor, I experienced serious complications which resulted in me having an emergency C-section. I was scared! My baby was fighting for her life inside of my womb! The umbilical cord was wrapped tightly around her neck three times! I had to trust that it was wrapped once for the Father, once for the Son, and once for the Holy Spirit. I knew God would never allow me to get on the birthing table only to lose my baby. And, like my God always does, He intervened, and His grace and mercy allowed my baby to catch her breath after the doctor unraveled the umbilical cord from around her neck. Once she caught her breath, that's when I caught mine. I hadn't even realized I was holding my breath while the doctors and nurses worked on Miracle. God is undoubtedly faithful to those who believe in Him. Shortly after baby Miracle was born, some of my family and close friends showed up at my hospital room. God kept his promise; I was not alone.

Reflecting back to last summer when Miracle was four months old, my children and I pulled up at a department store to go shopping. Once we arrived, I began having second thoughts about going in because India and Jacob expressed to me that they were getting hungry. Nevertheless, we entered into the store. Five minutes into us browsing, I spotted one of Mack's daughters, Kelsi, with her baby and Mack's ex-wife, Silvia. I recognized them from some pictures that he'd shared with me. I had been praying for God to provide a way for me to meet his older children with high hopes that Miracle could have a relationship with his side of the family. Never did I think that the opportunity would present itself in this way.

A feeling of total panic began to overtake me. I battled with myself as to whether or not I should approach them and introduce Miracle and myself. I feared being rejected and was unsure of what to say or how to handle what their reactions might be. I began to pray and ask God to give me the courage and strength to approach them, but my fear caused me to lose sight of Kelsi and Silvia. I continued to pray as my children and I walked around the store. God told me I had to approach them right then because the likelihood of me being able to experience an opportunity of that magnitude in the future might not exist again.

Finally, after the third time that I saw them in the store, I was ready to speak. Kelsi and her baby girl were in one part of the store and her mother, Silvia, was around the corner. The Lord told me to trust in Him, so I walked toward Kelsi and I introduced myself and Miracle to her. I felt tears welling up in my eyes as I experienced the emotion of the moment. A few minutes later, while I was giving Kelsi some background information about us, Silvia arrived. Kelsi told her mother who Miracle and I were. Both of them appeared concerned and presented a calm and pleasant demeanor.

I shared with Kelsi and Silvia that it was a prayer, and an important priority of mine for Miracle to have a fair chance of getting to know her father's family. Kelsi seemed interested in forming a relationship with Miracle and even asked to hold her baby sister. Kelsi mentioned to me that her baby and Miracle could be playmates; they were born just days apart. Kelsi and I agreed to keep in touch with each other as we exchanged phone numbers. We hugged and went in separate directions.

Less than thirty minutes after our departure, I received a phone call. It was Porsha, Mack's oldest daughter. She got my phone number from her sister, Kelsi. During our conversation, we arranged for Porsha to come over to our house to meet us. A couple of days later, Porsha came to visit us, and again, I was in tears from the exchange. My heart was full from the level of interest Porsha showed Miracle and me.

Porsha initially informed me that Kelsi was going to come over with her, but Kelsi ended up changing her mind and didn't show up. As we sat in my living room, Porsha told me she was interested in being a part of Miracle's life and that she would make an effort to connect my baby with their other family members. I asked if she could please take Miracle around Mack's siblings whom I met when we were dating. Porsha shared that she would be involved in Miracle's life; however, she could not speak for the rest of her family. She agreed to reach out to Mack's siblings regarding bringing Miracle around them. Porsha also told me she would let me know the next time she was going to babysit Kelsi's baby so that she and Miracle could play together.

Needless to say, Porsha did not keep her word, and to this day, none of what she said has manifested. For a very brief period, Porsha would reach out to me and check on Miracle. We were communicating on a regular basis at first. But then I began to notice a decline in Porsha's pattern of checking on Miracle. When I would call or text Porsha, it became consistent that she wouldn't respond. To date, Kelsi has not reached out to have a relationship with Miracle, and we've not seen or heard from her since a year ago when we met her at the department store. We have not met the third sister, Mya. I was under a false impression that this family was comprised of God-fearing Christians. I found it hard to understand how they could ignore their own blood by choosing not to form a bond with Miracle. To go about their lives as if she doesn't exist when they are fully aware of the fact that she does baffles me every day.

The challenges in my marriage, separating from my husband, then starting a relationship and having a baby with Mack were all pivotal points in my faith journey. I had to go through it all – every heartache, every tear, every gut-wrenching moment. I had to experience love and loss, joy and pain, and ultimately fear and faith. God showed me through my life's experiences that He would work everything out in His own timing and in His own unique way.

Now that Miracle is growing daily and becoming more aware, I am faced with knowing that one day she will ask me questions about her father. My heart is at peace because I will be able to tell her that her mommy tried to connect her with her father and his family, and I will remain open to Mack and his family being a part of her life if they choose. I will continue to trust in God while exercising faith. Throughout this journey, I will continue to believe and lean on God for peace, understanding, and protection. God has everything under control. He will fight our battles when we stand still and believe in His magnificent power to change our state of affairs. God also has His way of humbling even the toughest and most ego-centered souls. At last, I am letting go of this situation and letting God exert His will in the name of Jesus!

India, Jacob and Miracle fill my life with joy! Through my adversities, I have learned how to value quality over quantity as it relates to people in my life and in the lives of my children. I could not have asked for a better set of parents for my siblings and me. My daddy taught me how to be independent and to be able to stand on my own two feet, while having faith in the Lord. Because of my parents, and God, I have earned a Master's Degree, which has afforded me a career that allows me to take care of my babies with a greater sense of ease.

Having taken accountability for my actions in each of my experiences, I am now able to be a living testimony for other women who may be facing a similar storm. Having Fearless Faith does not mean that all trials and tribulations will suddenly dissipate from your life. Often times, situations will intensify before they level out. However, God equips believers with the necessary survival mechanisms to be able to rise above and press forward, in spite of. In living out Fearless Faith, I still face adversities. Now, rather than cripple myself to the fears that come with struggle, I view struggles as a temporary means to draw people permanently closer to God. Because of my past and present experiences, I have learned how to transform my struggles into my strengths. You, too, have the innate ability to do the same.

Building Your Fearless Faith Muscle:

1. Stand boldly and trust in God. He has the power to deliver you from unnecessary worrying and grant you the ability to focus on what is truly important in your walk of faith.

2. Courageously accept the challenges that God presents you with, for none of us are perfect. Have Fearless Faith in Him and believe that He will see you through your toughest circumstances.

3. Trust your God-given gift of discernment. When your spirit tells you something isn't right, trust your gut. God's gift of discernment lives deep inside of us, and when we activate our faith we are able to clearly hear from Him when something is right or wrong.

God Prevails

"Yet if any man suffer as a Christian, let him not be ashamed; but let him glorify God on this behalf."

1 Peter 4:16

As I sat on the airport shuttle bus on my way in to work, I wasn't sure what to think of the impossible that the state of Louisiana was about endure. I began to pray and call on God to keep my family and friends safe as I listened to the news on the shuttle bus radio. The newscaster stated that Hurricane Katrina had turned around in the Gulf of Mexico and was heading toward New Orleans. My mind was racing all over the place as I walked off the shuttle bus and in to work.

Three days later, the unthinkable happened - destruction beyond belief. Even though it has been twelve years, my heart still has a hole in it from the loss of loved ones that friends, and others endured during Hurricane Katrina. I can still see the dead bodies floating in the water and the New Orleans Armstrong Airport being made a morgue of people's loved ones. My God! My God!

When the storm was approaching, I was at work closing the stores and people were boarding the last flight out of Louisiana. My employer made reservations across the street at the Hilton Hotel for the employees and their families. They wanted us to ride out the hurricane out of harms' way. However, my family wanted to stay at home and did not come to the hotel with me, my husband and children. My parents always stayed home during major storms in the Saint Bernard Housing Projects located in New Orleans, Louisiana. This was the safest place to be than my own home in Marrero, Louisiana. Little did I know I would be separated from my parents, my siblings and niece and nephew.

When I arrived at the hotel I went straight to my room to take a shower, eat and get a little rest before the hurricane made landfall. I wanted to be up monitoring the weather and keeping in touch with my family and friends. When I spoke to my parents they stated that they were okay, and the worst of the hurricane was over. That the water only reached the bottom step of the front porch. I responded, "God is good! Amen." As I fell off to sleep I left my husband up watching the news. Then I felt a tap on my leg waking me up. It was morning. However, the look on his face told me something was very wrong. My husband made me promise I'd be okay before he told me to look at the news. Fear showed up for me that day. I know whatever it was, it was not going to be okay.

When I looked at the news, the Saint Bernard Housing Project was under water due to a levee giving way. I dropped to my knees with my mouth wide open, heart racing from anxiety and grabbing for my cell phone to call my parents. I desperately need to make sure they were okay. No answer. I could not breathe. I was screaming, "God why, why did you let this happen to my family?" God was telling me that it would be okay. But from what I was seeing on the news, it was not okay. I also thank God, every day that my baby was only one year old when Hurricane Katrina damaged Louisiana. He doesn't remember what we went through.

As my stomach was in a knot I could not eat or sleep without knowing what happened to my parents - my family. Still, God was telling me I needed to be strong for my family and that I was His child. He told me He would not leave me in my time of need. As I listened to God's word speak to my spirit I remembered summertime as a child when it was time to take a nap. It was so hot my mother used to put a blanket pad in the doorway of the front door – that way we could catch some breeze. She did the same thing when it would rain. I used to think I was dreaming when I looked out the screen door in the stormy rain and would see joyful visions of God smiling at me. My God! My God! I didn't realize God was watching over me then. When the Holy Spirit told me that I had the vision and wisdom that God gave me, now I see so clearly.

As the days went on, I still had no clue where my family was or if they were still alive. My heart was aching for my family. Here I was safe in a hotel with my husband and kids, when all the while I didn't know if my parents, siblings and niece and nephew were alive. Well, the hotel power went out and the backup generator was only going to last so many days. The meals were becoming less and less daily. My husband was finally able to contact his family in Thibodaux, Louisiana. They had lights and food, so we packed up the children and went there. Even in the comfort of my husband's family, I still couldn't sleep. I did not how many more I could endure. Then I heard word from my mother- in- law that a loved one had passed away due to taking sick during Hurricane Katrina. My heart dropped. This was a person that had been in my life since I was eighteen years old. I was devastated! I questioned God, "You told me it would be okay. Next will they tell me my family would not be found alive?" God told me to get plenty of rest and nourishment because I was about to endure the unthinkable. I needed to stay strong for my family.

Still wondering what happened to my family, one day I was sitting on the sofa and my niece texted me. She told me that a friend of their family saw her grandma and grandpa – my parents - in a shelter in Thibodaux, Louisiana. I responded, "What? You must be kidding me? I am in Thibodaux, Louisiana as well by my husband's cousins. I have been here for a week." God had placed my parents and family right down the road from me. My God! My God! I dropped to my knees and cried uncontrollably as nausea started to sit in the pit of my stomach. I rushed out of the house, jumped in the car and headed to Nicholls State University where the shelters were set up for displaced people. When I arrived and stepped inside, all I could see was my Mama, Daddy, sister, brother, niece and nephew sitting in the middle of the gym floor at Nicholls State University. They looked distressed due to the ordeal they had been through. As they looked up and saw us coming toward them, everybody hugged each other tight. I started bawling. I thought everybody was dead, but here I was now face to face with them. My family did not look well; they looked dehydrated and lacking nourishment. As we began to talk, they told me that they were rescued from the roof in a helicopter due to the Saint Bernard Housing Projects being under water. They lost everything, including their cars. You never know the true meaning of life until you have experienced disaster. My parents told me that the helicopter dropped them off on top of the Causeway Bridge which was the drop off sight. They were there for four days with no food or drink and no restrooms. They had to take turns wrapping a blanket around them to use the restroom in a bucket. My God! My God! Buses were finally able to come in and bus them to shelters, not knowing where the buses were going. But God had led them straight to me in Thibodaux. What an awesome God we serve!

My next game plan was getting them out of the shelter and checking on my property in Marrero, Louisiana. Three weeks later the curfew lifted only to let folks check on their property and then leave before 6:00 pm. So, as we drove from Thibodaux to Marrero, the damage I saw was unthinkable. When I arrived at my house it was still standing and had roof damage. Praise God it wasn't worse! I had to figure out a way to get the house cleaned out to move my family from the shelter.

Then, while standing in my driveway, I remembered exactly three weeks prior as I was getting ready for work around four in the morning I was scared to get in my car to leave for work. Usually my husband walks me out to my car, but I left him sleeping because he wasn't feeling well. So, I prayed and asked God to watch over me and get me in my car safely. No one was outside at the time, so I trusted God to keep me safe. God responded, "You don't need a man to watch over you. I am here my child. Go and get in your car. It will be okay. Have faith in me.

As I stepped outside and locked my door, I ran down the steps still looking around me in fear. Blind faith opened up the car door, put the keys in the ignition and started it up. I started to back out of the driveway. As I looked up, I hit the breaks to stop. There she was, an Angel standing in front of my car. She was glowing with wings. I knew I must have been dreaming. As I rubbed my eyes in disbelief and looked up again, she was gone. After that incident, I felt an ease of peace come over me, and I just smiled and went on my way to work.

When I got to work I told my staff what happened to me. They looked at me like I was crazy. That didn't matter to me. I had to call someone and tell them about my experience with the Angel. I called my brother and told him what happened. He said God was protecting me and my property for a reason. It all made sense. When Hurricane Katrina hit Louisiana, my house was the only one left standing. God, in His infinite wisdom, knew I had to get my family to safety. He knew my house would be here healing would begin. A prophet told me on a prayer call that an Angel was protecting my property, and she had her sword drawn I told the prophet my Angel was still there. God has allowed me to see His hand and His trust of me through the most powerful visions. Time passed; we were able to move home and take my family from the shelter.

Even though I had been praying all my life, I realized I had to learn *how* to pray. Yes, there is a difference. I used to pray for money, cars, jobs and health. Now I pray for God to give me wisdom, to lead me to my journey and show me my purpose and destiny. God, through prayer, has granted me the wisdom to elevate spiritually, professionally, physically and financially. After praying and believing, we heard from God. My family and I decided to leave the life we enjoyed for thirty years in Marrero and relocate to Plano, Texas.

Plano offered better jobs for me and my husband. We were excited for new opportunities and while praying, God revealed elevation for me if I would put my trust in Him. He encouraged me to stay focused and strong, no matter what obstacles we might come across. We knew it was going to be challenging, especially with no family in Plano, but we had no idea what we were to encounter. I have learned to be still and listen to God. Often, He speaks to me through a gospel song. He reminds me daily that He has always been there with me. I listened carefully as we prepared to make this major move. I had only one hesitation; leaving my parents and family. God assured me that they would be okay and reminded me again to stay focused.

We were excited as we packed several plastic crates, making sure to take everything we needed with us on our journey because we were moving from a house to an apartment. Even though I saw God's plans to elevate me, we were downsizing. Our plan was to lease an apartment for two years, learn the different cities for the best schools and then purchase another house. On our last scheduled Sunday at church, I intended to ask my brother, Pastor Chris Janeau, and sister, Cyntrell Janeau, if the choir could sing two of my favorite songs. However, with packing up the house and my desk at work, the time got away from me and I forgot to ask ahead. Sunday morning came, and we headed to church. On the drive, my thoughts and emotions were all over the place. I couldn't stop wondering if we were making the right decision. And my God, who is true to His word, spoke loud and clear that Sunday when the choir sang my two favorite songs without me having to ask. "Every Praise" and "It's Working," jolted me that day and clarified that my move to Texas was all part of God's larger plan for my life. So, we left all that we knew in Louisiana and headed to Texas.

The enemy is always busy trying to stop you from walking out your faith. We expected great things in Texas. We knew the journey wouldn't be easy, but we never expected what was to come. Within a few months after we relocated, the company my husband worked for was acquired by another company and he was laid off. We continue to soar and kept moving forward as I remembered God told me He would carry me through. I still had my job and my son was getting settled in school. My husband found a lower paying job with no health benefits, yet we kept pressing.

By this time, we had depleted most of our savings but not our faith that God would provide. I arrived home from work one day to find an eviction notice on the door. With tears burning my eyes, I looked up to the Heavens and said, "God, really? You promised me everything would be okay." I collected myself, so my husband wouldn't see the stress written on my face. How would we keep a roof over our heads and food on our table? Each day became a struggle, and to top it off, my husband took ill and had to stop working. He had no insurance to cover the medications for his diabetes, and my insurance wasn't trying to pay the four-hundred-dollar cost for one medication. I researched medication payment programs for low income families. My husband's doctor wrote a medical necessity letter, but the insurance company still refused to pay.

After three months without his medication, my husband developed severe nerve damage in his right arm and hand. I became angry with God. I began to question Him about what was happening to us. I asked, in doubt, "God how can I stay strong when we are not making ends meet financially?" I heard His still, small voice say, "I know you're hurting right now. But now is not the time to buckle. It's time for you to stay focused and be strong. You are my child and I have not forgotten you." I had to walk by faith and not by fear. The enemy knew I was scared, and he will always attack you at the deepest place of your fear and doubt. He studies us to know exactly where to throw his fiery dart. He even began threatening me in my dreams.

In one dream, I saw the devil standing in my kitchen. There were snakes wrapped tightly around my feet, and I woke up crying and screaming, yanking the covers off for fear they were the snakes taking hold of me. The Holy Spirit told me to go back to sleep, assuring me that He was beside me even in my dreams. The Holy Spirit also revealed to me during this time not to let anyone divide me and my husband – that we had to stay strong as a couple. I did not know I had entered spiritual warfare. The next day I called my brother, Chris, and shared with him my dream and what was going on in my life. He, like God, reminded me to stay strong and that this too would pass. My brother told me the devil had peeked into my future and was angry about what he saw. He was trying to break my faith in God. With everything else going on in my life, physically and financially during this time, I only confided in Christ, my Pastor my brother, Chris and my sister, Cyntrell. My sister-in- law, who I love like a sister, prayed with me for my family and also gave me the support I needed. Spiritual warfare was heavy in my life, and when you are on an assignment for God, it will attach itself to your life as well. It is up to us to understand and live by God's word. I knew I had to fight and could not give up because my family needed me.

We were in dire straits and ended up living in a drug and prostitute infested hotel for three weeks. Then, a woman named Beverly, who I thought was sent by God, allowed us to stay in her home. No one knew any of this was happening to my family. The Holy Spirit was warning me that something wasn't right about Beverly and that we needed to leave her home, but my family needed a roof over its head. I continued to search for an apartment and prayed God would show up quickly so that we wouldn't wear out our welcome in her home. Still, I felt uneasy there and couldn't figure out why. I prayed and asked God to reveal the enemy's plans, because I knew I had placed my family in enemy territory. All the while I could feel in my spirit that Beverly had a vindictive spirit toward me and meant to harm me, even while she smiled in my face. The Holy Spirit told me to go back to the apartment complex and speak to the manager. God confirmed we would have a home earlier than expected. The next day, while I was sitting at my desk at work, the manager of the apartment complex called and told me I could come and pick up my keys to move in. I went in the restroom and dropped to my knees thanking God. No one at my job knew what was going on with me and my family. I went to work every day with a smile on my face and always treated people the way I wanted to be treated. God told me no one needed to feel sorry for me because I was His child, and He would take care of me and my family. God revealed that my purpose in life is to help people that cannot help themselves. I had to go through every one of my storms so that God would strengthen me to help those He assigned to me – the homeless and the elderly. I realized God had never let me down. He always supplied what we needed. Through it all, He ensured one of us was employed.

After my family and I moved into our new apartment, it was then that the Holy Spirit revealed Beverly was going around telling lies and trying to damage my character with some co-workers and friends. Be mindful of those who invite you into their homes seemingly with no ulterior motives and no requests of you. Not everyone is bad, but sometimes the enemy will send wolves in sheep's clothing to bring harm to you and your family.

Walking in a life of faith means you must experience some things that show the power and presence of God in your life. My experience with Hurricane Katrina, loss of finances, relocating in doubt, my husband's illness and being evicted could have taken me out. But God! He is ever present and intentional, never failing. He cares about you. Be encouraged by the words He spoke to me and declare them as you pray for wisdom and spiritual growth in Him. Despite all I went through, God still had a plan for me. If God delivered Daniel in the lion's den, start envisioning what God will do for you as you walk through your adversities.

I ended up changing jobs once God reminded me He relocated me to Texas to elevate me and to help His people. My husband and I decided to start a non-medical transportation service to help the elderly people and to free up some time, so we could travel back home to see our parents and family that we missed dearly. I confided in a woman named Kenya. I had met her at my last from employer. Kenya had her own business and told me that she could start up the business for us, do the marketing, file the LLC paperwork, and find someone to write a grant for us. We had several meetings with her and everything seemed to be on the up and up. Then, I got that funny feeling in my spirit, similar to how I felt with Beverly. God was warning me to beware of familiar spirits. The startup cost was twelve hundred dollars, so we were to put down a six-hundred-dollar deposit, with the remaining six hundred dollars split into payments. I told Kenya my husband was out of work due to illness, and that I would take care of the payments for the start up. I paid the deposit by cashier's check and the remaining balance by money orders in order to have a paper trail of funds paid to her. All was going well. Kenya had even invited us to her wedding that suddenly got called off. I didn't think anything of it because life happens, and sometimes people have differences.

As it got closer to the time for me to make the last payment, I told her I need a few more months in order to pay. This startup was a financial sacrifice for us, and Kenya said that was fine because she knew what we were going through. Little did we know the entire time she was stealing our money. I should have seen it coming, especially when I got that uneasy feeling in my stomach. My husband would tell me all the time that people would take my kindness for weakness. That's what Kenya did! She spent so much time telling me about her problems that it distracted me from my money and business. Out of nowhere she told me she was taking a job in California and she was moving before the end of the year. I told her I would get my last payment together, so she could file for my LLC. Because she wore her Christianity like a coat on the outside, I didn't see the deceitfulness on the inside. A few days before Kenya left for California, she told me she filed my LLC paperwork. Something told me she wasn't telling me the truth, but I didn't press her. Two months passed, and I had not received anything in the mail from the State of Texas. I called her and questioned her about my paperwork. She claimed that due to her filing our paperwork toward the end of the year, it was probably being held up do to the State being busy end of year. This time, instead of allowing myself to believe her, I called the State of Texas to check if my LLC was filed under the business name. The representative told me when you file LLC paperwork it takes about a week to process before it's sent to you in the mail. The LLC had never been filed, and the representative confirmed my thoughts that Kenya had stolen our money. I confronted her about my call to the State and that I wanted our money returned. She lied and said she was putting it in the mail. We never received our money back from her, so I had to file charges with the police department against her. Of course, they couldn't locate her. The police department told me to file a civil case against her and make it public record so other people could be careful when doing business with her. What the enemy meant for harm, God turned it around in our favor. We never got our money back from her, but that didn't stop God from allowing us to start our business as well as several other businesses underway.

The enemy knows what God has in store for you. When you're under attack, that's a sure sign God is up to something amazing in your life. It wasn't easy, but I stayed strong and didn't allow my adversities to distract me from moving forward. I prayed for God to give me wisdom to recognize ungodly people, and God told me I had it in me all the time. I just had to make him first in my life in order to activate that part in my spirit that recognized deception. Now when an evil or deceitful person comes in my presence, I can feel their evil spirit and I ensure my whole armor of God is protecting me daily.

Find your fearless faith and your strength in I Peter 4:12-16: "BELOVED, THINK IT NOT STRANGE CONCERNING THE FIERY TRIAL WHICH IS TO TRY YOU, AS THOUGH SOME STRANGE THING HAPPENED UNTO YOU. But rejoice, in as much as ye are partakers of Christ's sufferings; that, when his glory shall be revealed, ye may be glad also with exceeding joy. If ye be reproached for the name of Christ, happy are ye; for the spirit of the glory and of God in others resteth upon you: on their part he is evil spoken of, but on your part he is glorified. But let none of you suffer as a murderer, or as a thief, or as an evildoer, or as a busybody in other men's matters. Yet if any man suffer as a Christian, let him not be ashamed; but let him glorify God on this behalf."

As I close my chapter, I am reminded that the goodness of God was always with me and my family, and I had to really listen and receive it. God wants it all for His children. He wants you to love him with a pure and clean heart and soul. Remember while you are going through the storm that God delivered me, and your Fearless Faith will suddenly activate because you know He has already delivered you. Believe in advance for your breakthrough. God Prevails! Trials and trouble are a test of your faith, and when you come through the storm, stand strong. Everyone's trials and troubles are different because God made each one of us different. Your walk through the storm may not be my walk through the storm. But, trust me when I say, you will come out of your storm unharmed.

Fear was my culprit and almost stopped me from moving forward to achieve the blessings that God had for me and my family. But, when I charged my faith batteries, Fearless Faith stepped in, God took over, and I was able to relax into the splendor of His grace and mercy for my life.

I pray this book touches someone or helps someone move closer to God's direction because he loves you unconditionally and He is intentional. BE BLESSED!

Building Your Fearless Faith Muscle

1. Press forward and stay strong. Many times, I wanted to give up but, instead, I stayed prayed up and I didn't listen to others that didn't have my best interest at heart.

2. Pray and ask God to show you and give you the wisdom you need to protect you and your family because spiritual warfare is real, and so many people do not recognize it. Never be afraid to have a talk with Him, not only in your time of need but thank him even in your time of abundance. When you meditate on His word and know who you are in Him, He will ensure there is never any lack in your household.

Lessons Learned

"And He said to me, "My grace is sufficient for you, for My strength is made perfect in weakness.""

II Corinthians 12:9

As I sat and heard the words coming from my boss's mouth, all my feelings and emotions seemed to leave my body. I was numb. I felt as if someone had sucked all the life out of me.

The last time I felt this way was when I got the news my Mother had died or maybe the afternoon of my Father's death. Or maybe it was that pre-dawn call I received one Friday that my brother had crashed on his motorcycle. Or perhaps it was when I arrived at the scene to see him lying in the street covered up and knowing what the police were about to come and tell me.

Each of those times I felt lifeless. I felt like I would never be able to breathe again. I felt I would forever be stuck in that horrible moment. On August 27, 2015, I didn't think I would live to see August 28, 2015.

I was released from the company I had given 16 ½ years of service. I was terminated from the company I had planned to retire from within the next five to eight years. I was fired from AT&T because of a code of business conduct violation.

I had been unemployed before. But, to be fired, let go at this stage in my life? How would I survive? Would I be able to bounce back? Being a woman of faith, my mind said, "*Of course*," but in my head at that moment, I really wasn't sure. Honestly, I was full of fear not faith.

Immediately, I thought of my daughter and my significant other. How would I tell them the meeting didn't go as we planned or prayed it would? How, and what, would I tell them? Those two conversations were extremely difficult, but with God's grace, I told them. They were both extremely loving and encouraging. They both reminded me this too would pass. My daughter took it a step further and reminded me the situation didn't catch God by surprise (something I often told her).

Soon, the word was out I was looking for another job. Each time I told the story, it seemed even more unreal to me. Some were encouraging. Some were hopeful. Some reminded me God would take care of me. However, others were shocked. Some were disappointed. They couldn't believe "Minister Debra", "Intercessor Debra", "Servant/Servant Leader Debra" had been terminated because of an integrity issue.

I felt all the above and then some. I had parents who loved me and sacrificed so I could go to college; but instead of finishing my education, I decided to get married. Even after their deaths, I received at various intervals, cash from different things they had set up for me. I didn't invest or spend wisely and soon I would find myself in debt again. All of these thoughts kept coming up while trying to focus on securing employment.

I didn't think finding another job would be that difficult. I had great skills. I knew people who were in position to make things happen or influence decision makers. It was hard NOT to find a company advertising an administrative position. Soon I would learn it was even harder to be placed in one of those jobs. Many told me it was time for me to walk out my calling, to live on purpose, to pursue my passion. There was a slight problem. I had no clue how any of that translated into dollars and cents.

I couldn't see myself making a living off any of that. I wasn't that talented. I wasn't…well… I wasn't anything, and I certainly wasn't factoring God into ANY of this.

I sent out resume after resume. I contacted and signed up with temporary personnel agencies. I used my network of friends and family. My daughter even started reaching out to people on my behalf. Email after email I received, 'Thanks but no thanks!" And those were the ones where people took the time to respond. Being unemployed started to take its toll on me. I was emptying out accounts left and right. Every nest egg I had didn't just crack, they were totally broken and used up.

My faith walk took a hit, too. I went to church. I continued serving. Whatever monies I received, I continued to tithe. I even attempted to give more whenever I could. I was determined to continue loving and serving God. Yet, the more the rejection letters, emails and calls came, the less hopeful I felt. I pushed myself; but honestly, I felt my faith crumbling underneath me. I started questioning God. Because I knew He was in control and He knew the beginning and the end, I questioned Him as one who had all power and authority. However, the longer I went through, I started questioning God in a way that caused even me to wonder, where was my faith? It started to feel like I'd thrown my faith in a pot of boiling water and forgot about it, causing the water to boil out and burn my faith to the bottom of the pot.

My confidence and self-esteem took a tremendous blow. Suddenly, instead of seeing myself as God did, I started seeing myself as the enemy did. I was a failure. I was full of fear. I felt employers saw me as too old and unable to learn new things. I feared more than anything else I had reached my destination in life, and it wasn't how I had planned.

I started comparing myself to others who had gone through this. If we had 99 things in common, I would pick the one thing we didn't share and focus on why that one thing would keep me from being successful. I started to become withdrawn. My fear was starting to paralyze me. During this time, I started walking at a lake near my house. I would get up faithfully three to four times per week, walk and listen to my music. I loved my morning walks and talks with God. But soon, my newfound companion - the enemy - found a way to disrupt my peace.

One morning I was looking down at the lake feeling peaceful and taking in God's creation. Almost immediately I started thinking about how after two months I STILL didn't have a job. For some, two months may seem like a short time. For me, it felt like an eternity. I realized out of all the temporary agencies I had signed up for, none had called me with an assignment. I thought about how my daughter depended on me. She was in her last year of college; but honestly, I had no idea how we would get that last semester paid for. It had started to become a struggle to pay bills. How had I ended up here? God, I pondered, what are you trying to teach me? Why am I hurting so much? In addition to the questions mounting, I felt guilt and shame. The voice in my head seemed to get louder. I kept hearing, *"You are a failure."* I felt I had let down God, my daughter, my significant other, and all those who loved me. I thought of the women I mentored and ministered to, and I felt like a fraud. I thought of my parents (both deceased) and how they did all they could to make sure I had the necessary tools to be successful in life. Yet, instead of taking advantage of my opportunities, I had blown them all. By now the tears streaming down my face were uncontrollable. Why should I continue to go on? Instead of helping others I was hurting them. I felt people looked at me with pity, disdain and disgust.

Standing at the dam, I looked down at the lake. I was trying to gather up the courage to take the plunge. *"If I just jump right now,"* I told myself, *"I could end it all."* I couldn't take what I was experiencing any longer. As I stood on the bank, I heard God's voice clearly. He reassured me He had forgiven me. He reassured me He still loved me; and then He reminded me of my worth. He told me I was still His child. I was still His chosen vessel, and He was still in control of my life. At the end of that lake, His final words to me were, "Do you trust Me?"

While standing there, still not quite sure what my next move would be, a song came on my playlist startling me. The song was, "Love Lifted Me." It was so befitting for the moment. As I listened to the words of the song, the tears of sadness turned into tears of joy. The song playing was a reprise of another song, "Worth" by gospel artist Anthony Brown & group therAPy. The words of the song soothed me and drowned out the negative thoughts. God's love lifted me out of that dark place I was in. Reminding myself of the sacrifice He made for me to be free was all I needed to begin pulling myself together.

Each time I heard the phrase, love lifted me, I could feel myself being lifted. I felt my spirit being set free. I heard God remind me that nothing I could do would separate His love from me. He reminded me I was still a mother, a minister, a mentor, and because of Him I mattered. I left the lake feeling encouraged. I left the lake knowing everything was going to be all right. I left the lake ready to find and start my new job.

But life can sometimes be a series of ebbs and flows. Soon after that day at the lake, I started a new job; a place where real ministry went forth. I went to work each day with a joyful and grateful heart for God allowing me to be a part of this awesome experience. After only a few months on the job, I felt a shift – a shift in the wrong direction. One night, I dreamed about being released from that job. It wouldn't be long before my dream became a reality. Again, I was faced with decreasing resources. And again, God kept reminding me HE was my source and all I needed.

My daughter went back to school for her final semester. Her financial aid package for the Spring semester looked bleak. BUT GOD! A few days before the semester started, she was blessed with some extra aid because of her status as a senior. Both of us rejoiced in knowing God as a provider. It was four months before I found steady work again. When I worked for AT&T, I could pretty much tell you the exact time my paycheck would be deposited in my account. I knew the amount almost to the penny. I desperately needed that type of assurance again. God kept reminding me - He was in the driver's seat and I needed to let Him take control. I ended up getting a temporary assignment, which after 30 days working, my assignment ended. To say I was devastated was an understatement. On top of my troubles, it seemed as if my daughter was starting to be affected by what I was experiencing. The day of her graduation, she was offered a job a few miles from the house. The salary was excellent. But a few weeks later, she found herself trying to figure out what her Plan B was going to be. This put even more pressure on me to practice what I preached. I tried to live my faith out loud, but my fears overwhelmed me. I did all I knew to do, including seeking God daily. I studied the scriptures. I listened to sermons. I hung on to every word of hope I could get. I prayed like never before. But, still no job. My 401k was gone. My unemployment was gone. The bills were steadily increasing. But as much as God was allowing MY resources to dry up, He would send people to bless me. Just when I wondered how I would have enough to pay a bill, somebody would walk up to me and hand me cash or a check. Or I would receive a phone call saying what can I pay for you this week? This was a new experience for me.

God also blessed my daughter like only He can. She was notified by her alma mater of an available position and the opportunity for her to work on her Master's Degree. While an undergraduate, we struggled as to how we would pay the balance due each semester; and now she was given an opportunity to obtain a free Master's Degree! It was during this time, I learned to trust God like never before. It had been 18 months since I last had a steady job with benefits. There were times when I wondered if I would ever have that again.

I had Type II Diabetes, hypertension, and high cholesterol. I needed to be on medication. The Affordable Health Care insurance wasn't very affordable for me. I prayed for my healing. My significant other and I had decided we were going to get married. However, my debt was extremely high and my income was almost non-existent. It was a real concern. Especially knowing most marriages that end in divorce end because of finances. I prayed. He prayed. We prayed.

Our story was already amazing (to us anyway). We had dated 18 years prior. Our breakup was simply two people moving in different directions. We remained casual friends. When we started dating again, we decided early on marriage was our goal. The plan was for us to work a few more years; build up our retirement accounts; pay down our debt and then he would retire first and me shortly thereafter. But now that I couldn't seem to buy a job, those plans weren't falling into place. He helped me financially. However instead of things getting better, it was like we were both drowning. If things were like this now, what would it be like when we got married? Better? Worse? Only God knew.

After much prayer and counsel, we united in holy matrimony on November 26, 2016. Another faith walk. Our decision to get married was based on our love for each other and our faith in God. We believed that God had reconnected us after so many years, that we were destined to be together. We trusted God in taking this next step in our relationship, and we wanted God to bless our union.

After the wedding, I just knew my next opportunity was right around the corner. There were days we felt as if we were standing in quicksand dying a slow death. But we trusted and believed in God and each other. And I can truly say God has kept us. Five months after we got married and 20 months after AT&T, God blessed me with exceedingly and abundantly more than I could ask or think. He opened a door for me to once again work for a Fortune 500 company. A steady job with great benefits AND I could work from home. All the things I asked God for during my private prayer time, He responded to favorably. I had to totally surrender and trust Him completely. In a surrendered state, I was in the right position to receive the blessings of God. During this time, I learned God is truly my source. I said it many times; but after 20 months, I knew it without a shadow of doubt. I learned without faith it is impossible to please God. While challenges caught me off guard at times, nothing catches God by surprise. When I put my faith, trust and hope in Him; He would not lead me astray. I learned even though I'm not always faithful to Him, He who promises is faithful! I learned God loves me beyond measure. I learned His love could lift me from the deepest depths of despair. I learned His love could turn my tears of sadness into tears of joy in a matter of minutes.

I learned Romans 8:28 (NKJV), *"And we know that all things work together for good to those who love God, to those who are the called according to His purpose."*

I learned Jeremiah 32:17 (NKJV) *"Ah, Lord God! Behold, You have made the heavens and the earth by Your great power and outstretched arm. There is nothing too hard for You."*

Going through it was not easy. But because I pressed through, I give God praise, honor and glory. I now know Him in a different way.

I learned First Peter 1:6-7 (NKJV) *"In this you greatly rejoice, though now for a little while, if need be, you have been grieved by various trials, 7 that the genuineness of your faith, being much more precious than gold that perishes, though it is tested by fire, may be found to praise, honor, and glory at the revelation of Jesus Christ,"*

I learned Jeremiah 29:11 (NKJV) *"For I know the thoughts that I think toward you, says the Lord, thoughts of peace and not of evil, to give you a future and a hope."*

I learned Philippians 4:6-7 (NKJV) "Be anxious for nothing, but in everything by prayer and supplication, with thanksgiving, let your requests be made known to God; 7 and the peace of God, which surpasses all understanding, will guard your hearts and minds through Christ Jesus."

I learned Psalm 84:11 (NKJV). *"For the Lord God is a sun and shield; The Lord will give grace and glory; No good thing will He withhold from those who walk uprightly."*

I learned Second Corinthians 12:9 (NKJV) *"And He said to me, "My grace is sufficient for you, for My strength is made perfect in weakness." Therefore, most gladly I will rather boast in my infirmities, that the power of Christ may rest upon me."*

I learned Ephesians 2:8-9 (NKJV). *"For by grace you have been saved through faith, and that not of yourselves; it is the gift of God,"* I'm thankful for His grace that saved me!

Because of my experiences, I can now boldly share with others that what God did for me He can and will do for them. God is no respecter of person. I learned during those 20 months to keep seeking Him during the down times.

I learned Hebrews 11:6 NKJV. "……. *God is a rewarder of those who diligently seek Him.*" During my time of trial and testing, I'm grateful I kept seeking Him.

I learned Hebrews 11:1-2, NKJV. *"Now faith is the substance of things hoped for, the evidence of things not seen. 2 For by it the elders obtained a good testimony." (Hebrews 11:1-2 NKJV)*

A few weeks after my lake experience, I envisioned myself sharing my testimony. There is no testimony without a test. And, the greater the test the greater the testimony! And because of the lessons learned; my understanding of what NOW faith is; and my new revelation of Him, I'm now sharing my good testimony. God, in His sovereignty, taught me how to move from being a woman of fear, to a woman full of faith and now a woman who possesses fearless faith!

Building Your Fearless Faith Muscle:

As I reflect over this season of my life, I'm encouraged because I learned to grow through what I was going through. It wasn't easy and at times; I wanted to give up. But God! He gave me sufficient grace to complete this journey and test of faith. As a result, I moved from having a weak, underdeveloped faith muscle, to becoming a woman of fearless faith with a strong faith muscle.

When a person wants to develop muscle in their body, there is no hard and fast rule to accomplish this feat. It takes time, effort and hard work. There are drugs that can enhance the process; but the desired result may be flawed, or other problems may occur due to using these methods. Daily activities of weight lifting exercises, eating protein, and getting proper rest are listed in almost any 'how to develop muscle' guide.

For me, I found the following crucial to develop, build and strengthen my faith muscle:

1. Reading God's Word - Studying, knowing and hearing the Word of God helped me daily. On the days I was at my weakest, applying the Word of God to my situation encouraged and helped me to endure.

Listening to or reading sermons, reading and studying the written Word of God, or just pulling certain scriptures from my memory bank helped tremendously. I was encouraged when I learned and/or was reminded what others had gone through or were going through similar situations or worse. Being reminded God is able; He is no respecter of person; what He did for others He could and would do for me, gave me hope that I, too, would overcome. *"And they overcame him by the blood of the Lamb and by the word of their testimony, and they did not love their lives to the death." Revelations 12:11 NKJV*

2. Remembering God's Promises - Studying the Word, I was also reminded of the Promises of God. The Bible is filled with many promises to the believer. Even when we fall, God is there to pick us up and draw us back to Him. The key is for us to be willing to allow Him to work in and through us. Reading and being reminded of His promises helped me to be strengthened. Even though my situation seemed terminal; even though my situation seemed hopeless; God's promise to finish the work He had begun in me allowed me to keep pressing. *"Being confident of this very thing, that He who has begun a good work in you will complete it until the day of Jesus Christ;" Philippians 1:6 NKJV "I press toward the goal for the prize of the upward call of God in Christ Jesus." Philippians 3:14 NKJV*

3. Receiving God's Plans - I am a student of Bible Study Fellowship. Almost each week during this season, our teaching leader would remind us the plans of God cannot be thwarted. No man can stop God's plans. We may get detoured, delayed, or misdirected but His purpose for us would be fulfilled. The Children of Israel embarked on a journey to The Promised Land that should have lasted days but ended up taking 40 years. Their disobedience and disbelief caused a deliberate and divine delay by God. They failed to receive God's plan for their life. However, they did reach the Promised Land just as God said. So it was for them, so it was for me. God's purpose and plans for my life were not changed. Learning from the delays, learning to believe and not doubt, learning to trust

and obey, learning to receive God's plan for my life in spite of what my current circumstances were, caused my faith muscle to be strengthened. It was strengthened because God is a promise keeping God, and what He has planned and purposed for me will come to pass. *"I know that You can do everything, And that no purpose of Yours can be withheld from You." Job 42:2 NKJV*

CHAPTER 5
PAULA BRADLEY

Surviving Through a Painful Process

"There hath no temptation taken you but such as is common to man: but God is
faithful, who will not suffer you to be tempted above that ye are able; but will
with the temptation also make a way to escape, that ye may be able to bear it."
1 Corinthians 10:13

My life did not go as I had envisioned as a little girl. My initial hopes and
dreams were to finish high school, go away to college, get a degree and one
day become a nurse. I also wanted to be a single, successful woman traveling
the world and experiencing life. I would wait until I was older and settled to
get married and have children. I wanted the big house, a huge yard and to
live comfortably. However, life doesn't always turn out the way we want it to.

I had my first child at sixteen years old, in the 11th grade. Of course,
that wasn't part of the vision, but it happened. I still went to school and
was able to graduate with my class. This definitely wasn't an easy journey.
Having the responsibility of taking care of a little life when I couldn't even
take care of myself was challenging then, and I'm sure it would be even more

challenging now. There were many days after being up all night with a crying baby that I wanted to quit school, give up and throw in the towel. But thank God for supportive parents that continued to push me and encouraged me to stay focused and hang in there. Because with them, quitting school was not an option.

Like some of my classmates, I didn't get to go away to college after graduating high school. I attended community college and took online courses to continue my education. The Marvin, the father of my child wanted to marry me and raise our child together. I believed this was the right thing to do. After all, I didn't make this baby by myself. I thought things would be easier because I wouldn't be a single parent. It certainly wasn't my parents' responsibility to take care of our child. As a teenager, I had made some life-changing decisions, and I needed to take responsibility for those decisions. My plans could no longer go as I had envisioned when I was a young girl. They had to be altered.

Well, my marriage to Marvin lasted only about two years. Although we tried, we were both too young, and neither of us knew what we were doing. Times were hard for us. We weren't able to keep a roof over our heads, food to eat, a car to drive, pay daycare and take care of our baby girl, so we finally decided that we needed to do something different. Our young marriage ended in divorce. I went back to live with my parents, and we continued to provide for our daughter who is now an adult and an awesome woman of God.

Two years later I got involved with David who would become my second husband. We hadn't been dating long before I got pregnant with my second child, a beautiful baby girl. It would be nearly thirteen months to the day, I became pregnant with my son. My children were the best thing to come out of the marriage. If it wasn't for my children, I believe I would live in constant regret of ever meeting him because of all of the lying and cheating in the marriage. If I had to do it all over again, I would change the way I viewed myself at that time. I didn't believe I was worthy of love and I accepted less than I thought I deserved. But my children are a blessing to me, and the loves of my life and there is absolutely nothing that I wouldn't do for them.

David and I dated for several years before we were married. We lived in the same neighborhood, and we were fellowshipping under the same leadership. He couldn't be too bad, right? Well, things aren't always what they appear to be, and neither are people.

We dated and lived together for several years off and on before we were married. Our dating years weren't nice at all. Initially I thought I was the only woman in his life. After being with him for a while I learned that there were at least two other women. Throughout those years there were constant lies, infidelity, deceit and betrayal. David knew all the right things to say and could lie his way out of anything. He knew exactly what to do to keep me right where he wanted me. He knew he had my heart and he took advantage of that.

After our last breakup and several conversations, he asked me to marry him. He had asked several times before, but I had declined. Although I wanted to marry him, I was fearful that he would continue the same behavior. After months of reassuring me that he had changed - that he was ready to be totally committed to me, I reluctantly said yes." There was still a lack of trust in my heart, but I had no proof of anything and my husband had been pouring his heart out to me. Call me crazy if you must, but in the words of Bishop T. D. Jakes, "keep talking and keep living because life will surely shut your mouth."

I had been a single parent for several years maintaining food, clothing, shelter and all the essentials for me and my children, and I was tired of doing it by myself. I was tired of being the head of my household and paying all the bills. I had children by two different men and I at least wanted them to grow up with one of their fathers in the house. Single parenting was no joke and I also didn't want my children to grow up in a single-parent home. And they didn't. They grew up in a home where much of the time only one parent was actively involved.

Yes, I had a support group of friends, family and other people around me that loved me, but I still felt alone and lonely in my situation. I wasn't trusting God, so I responded out of desperation and stepped outside of His will for my life.

What I didn't know was that marrying this man would be the beginning of the most painful season of my life and that it would damage me in a way I never dreamed of. I made a huge mistake. I didn't realize it then, but I know it now.

Did I pray about this decision before going into it? Yes. I confess; however, that I didn't wait on an answer from God. I guess I knew He would say no. It's a dangerous thing to step ahead of God. Although He had my best interest in mind and He knew this was not what He had for me, He gave me the freedom of choice. I chose this situation. For years I felt that God was punishing me for walking in disobedience. I stayed in it because I felt it was what I deserved, and I had no right to walk out.

This is what happens when we move outside of God's order, when we remove him out of the equation and allow our flesh to jump on the throne. Flesh wants what flesh wants and if we do not bring it under subjection to the word and the will of God, it will rule and super-rule us. It will have us tied up with people that God didn't ordain to be in our lives.

My husband and I got married and within the first six months of our marriage my husband told me he was called into the ministry to preach the gospel. My mind was rambling, "What? Are you kidding me? Oh Lord, what have I gotten myself into? Me, a preacher's wife? Is this why he married me? Was it because he wanted to be married before he accepted his calling and he thought I was the best candidate for this assignment? I don't know if I'm ready for this. On second thought is he ready for this? Is he sure about this? This is not what I signed up for." It completely caught me off guard because I had never envisioned myself as a preacher's wife. I believe it was in April of that following year that he received his license to preach.

The first two or three years of marriage, as far as I can recall, were okay, or at least I told myself they were. My husband was taking care of the family, we were walking in agreement, I was happy to be married and to have someone to share my life with other than my children. To start fresh, we moved from the house where I had been living to another house where we lived for about two years. Then we purchased our first home. Things seemed to be headed in the right direction. We were serving in ministry at the church and I was experiencing a life of fulfillment. Ministry has always been my passion. It's what I love to do and there is no greater reward for me than when I have been instrumental in leading someone to Christ.

A few years later my then-husband was ordained as a minister, which was an even greater calling and responsibility in ministry. This would require more time and commitment from both of us. I didn't want to do anything that would hinder the ministry. I didn't know if I was prepared to take on such a sacred calling. Although I wasn't a minister of the gospel at that time, I was to be by my husband's side supporting him in the ministry. I felt inadequate and unequipped. So, I prayed and expressed my concerns to the Lord. I asked God to help me to fulfill the assignment that He had placed on me. God assured me that those he calls, He equips (Hebrews 13:21). He had prepared me for such a time as this.

For a while, things were still going okay. Over the next few years my husband became a long-distance truck driver, so there were many periods that I was home alone with the children. We had four children by then; we were also raising our daughter from his previous marriage. Again, I felt like a single parent. When there were school programs, I was the parent that attended. When there was football, basketball, track (you name it), I was there. Parent conferences, you got it, there I was. I'm not knocking it or complaining; this was the joy of parenting and investing time and energy in my children. My complaint was my husband's paycheck did not add up to his time spent on the road. Sometimes he was away for a couple of weeks, but his check was never enough to cover his portion of the bills. I never knew what he made, and I never saw one of his paychecks. He gave me what he wanted me to have, and I had to take care of the rest to make up the difference.

He began spending more and more time away from me, and the children. Even on his days off, he was never home. I caught him in several lies and began receiving hang-up phone calls. There were times when our phone would ring and if I answered it, the person on the other end would not say anything. Others would tell me that they had seen him with our women. Any time I questioned him, it turned into an argument. The deceit, betrayal and signs of infidelity had returned. Yes, I experienced it while we were dating and again while we were married. Although I knew it was possible, I didn't truly expect to have to face this. We had taken an oath before God and witnesses to be committed to each other until death.

I petitioned God with my concerns because I knew that He would hear me, and He wouldn't judge me. I was safe sharing my heart with Him. He was the only one that could change my husband, change my situation and give me the strength to endure until the change came. I prayed, "Lord, you know exactly what I'm going through right now. What have I done to deserve this treatment? Why doesn't he love me? This hurts so badly. What am I supposed to do? Do I continue to stay in it because I chose this? Lord, I need direction."

I had many questions, but no clear answers, no clear direction. I was in a painful place and didn't want anyone to know. I certainly couldn't allow my children to see me upset and crying all the time. I didn't share with my family because I didn't want them involved. I was afraid that if my friends knew all the crap I was going through, they would look at me differently.

I don't believe my husband knew what he was doing to me and to our family. He was busy perfecting his image and camouflaging by taking care of everyone else. His family was falling apart while he kept up the appearance of perfection.

I believe emotional abuse is one of the worst kinds of abuse. In no way do I minimize the effects of physical abuse because abuse is abuse and it has a very negative impact. However, if you hit me, people can see the bruises and the scars. If you verbally abuse me, people can hear that. But if I were being abused emotionally, you would never know unless I shared it with you. Only the Lord and I knew about it. There's no outside evidence because every pain is within.

Many nights I would lie on my bedroom floor, bawling from frustration, asking God to take me out. I remember telling God if this is how I must live my life I no longer wanted to live. "Just take me NOW!" I was just so tired of trying to keep things together, pretending that everything was okay when my house was a mad house.

This mad house extended to those outside of our homes. Many of our acquaintances did not want our marriage to work. From day one, they said it wouldn't last. The tongues of some church folks can be as venomous as snakes. It was my goal to prove them wrong. But it seemed he was giving them just what they wanted. Ironically, we were part of the leadership team for the marriage ministry. I knew he was hearing the same word that I was hearing, but I couldn't understand why nothing seemed to change. What was wrong with this dude? Everyone else's marriage seemed happy. What was wrong with us? Why couldn't we be happy? I became jealous of those around me that seemed to be happily married. I say *seemed* because I didn't go home with them. I was a faithful wife; I took care of my home and my children. Why was the Lord allowing my marriage to be in turmoil?

I didn't journal much, but on March 21, 1999 I wrote in my journal:

"Lord, I really need to get this out of me. You are the only one that I feel really understands me. You said in 1 Peter 5:7 that I could cast my cares on you because you care for me. I went to church this morning wearing another mask to come home to the same old crap. Why is this happening to me? I only want what you said I'm supposed to have. That is a husband that loves me like you love the church and gave yourself for it (Ephesians 5:25). I'm tired of being a trophy wife when he wants to look good in front of people. I've had to endure so much heartache and pain throughout this marriage. I don't even think he knows who I am anymore. Love, I don't even believe he knows what that is. I just don't understand what I'm supposed to do. I'm tired of being mistreated and walked on like a door mat. I'm tired of the emotional abuse. There must be something better for me. Lord, I'm sorry; please forgive me for walking outside of your will and walking in disobedience. Lord, have mercy on me and please HELP."

Time and time again the craziness continued. I would leave; he would ask me to come back, saying things would be different. In reality, I didn't leave; I just changed my address for a few days. My heart still lived at my old address. I didn't want to uproot my children. I thought about them having to change schools and what a serious relocation would do to them. I wanted them to have a stable environment. The environment that offered residential stability was emotionally unstable for all of us. I didn't think I could stop loving this man. Was it really love that I had for him? I don't know. But I would always go back.

It didn't get better, it actually got worse. One day my son and I were riding in the car when I received a call from my daughter asking where we were. I could tell that there was a concern, so I asked her what was going on. She informed me that she had just seen her dad pulling into a hotel. She was on a volunteer assignment and was riding on a van with other volunteers. She provided me with the exact location of the hotel. Me, not really thinking about the impact that this might have on my son; I turned the car around and went directly to the hotel. Upon locating my husband's car, I sat there waiting for someone to come out of one of the two doors that were directly in front of the two cars. While waiting I took pictures of the hotel and both cars. I called our pastor to come and meet me at the hotel. My heart raced; I had never been in this position before. I didn't know exactly what I was going to do or how this was going to turn out. I looked at my son who sat and watched innocently. I wished I hadn't brought him with me, but we were there, and I didn't have anyone to call to come get him. I didn't want to leave because I thought if I caught my husband in the act that it would cause him to repent and make a change. Finally, the female walks out of the room, recognizes me, jumps in her car and drives off. Meanwhile I'm taking pictures of her because it was my plan to send them to her husband. Yes, this was a married woman that my husband was sleeping with. I proceeded to go into the hotel room finding my husband half-dressed. While waiting for our pastor to arrive I began asking my husband what he was doing here. This dude totally denied that anything had happened and even tried to convince me that I was crazy because there was never a woman in the room. His explanation was that he came there to rest because I would not keep our teenage children quite at home so that he could sleep. Really?

Finally, our pastor arrived, and my husband repeated the same lies to him. I'm not sure why it surprised me, but I never thought he would lie when the truth was starring him in the face. When I could no longer deal with this fiasco, I left. I went home packed my bags and went to my parents for a few nights. I was truly at a crossroads in my life and in my marriage. Again, I returned home to the same old drama.

I was on the road to an emotional and mental breakdown. There were days that I would go to work and point out women that I thought were very nice looking. I would say to myself, "that is a woman that my husband would have an affair with." I didn't realize until much later that my self-esteem had been demolished and I was tormenting myself.

We counseled with some Christian leaders, but still nothing changed. I was starting to hate my husband for what he was doing, and that scared me. I wished something would happen to him so that he could feel what I was feeling. There were several occasions when other men approached me. However, I loved my husband; I was dedicated first to God, then to him. Just because he was cheating didn't give me the right to cheat. I know you're saying if there was infidelity according to the scripture I had all rights to exit. That's true, but considering the pattern I established, I was afraid to leave without being completely sure that God had given me permission. I couldn't allow myself to listen to others. I had to be sure that I heard from God. When I left this time, I never wanted to come back again. This had become my place of pain.

January 31, 2005, not really knowing how all of this would turn out I took assurance of faith in God and left. Only one friend knew the day that I planned to move. I didn't want it said that my family tore my marriage apart. No, this was between him and me. This, I wanted to do on my own.

The three girls had either gone to college or moved out. It was only my son and I. The children had walked this journey with me. I did everything within my power to keep the pain of the journey hidden, but they were aware of my unhappiness. During the years that they were in the house they did witness some things. My son probably suffered the most and witnessed so much that he should not have. He witnessed me going from strip clubs to hotels only to find his dad in compromising positions with other women. Part of me believes he knew and saw more things than that, but I never asked him. All of this affected him in a devastatingly negative way. He dropped out of school, got involved with gangs, stealing and doing things that were totally out of character from the son I had raised. Eventually, all of his troubles cost him ten years lost behind prison walls.

My life had flat lined. It felt like I'd come to the end of my road. My life had forever changed. I was angry with myself and felt responsible for all my son had experienced. I believed that if I had done things differently, maybe God would have done something differently. I repeatedly asked, "God, where are you?" The "old folks" would say, "You don't question God." But, I had to. I needed answers that wouldn't come soon.

I remember closing the door on what once was home for me. Closing that door was symbolic of closing that chapter of my life. It was bittersweet. Although I was about to begin a new chapter, this was my life, as I had known it. This is where I raised my children, but this was also my place of pain and agony.

I settled in my new place ready to move forward with exiting the marriage and beginning my new single life. I thought that things would get better, but they didn't, at least not immediately. Living alone was uncomfortable for me because I had always lived with other people in my house. I missed my son who had begun to exhibit behavioral problems and was not with me. My children were always there. Now it was just me.

February 2005 at four o'clock in the morning I woke up. My heart was racing. My stomach was upset. I was scared. I was having an anxiety attack. I had never experienced this before; I thought I was having a heart attack. I got up, went to the bathroom and grabbed my Bible. I turned to Psalms 91 and began to read it repeatedly. I claimed these words over my life because I honestly thought I was dying. The devil had attacked not only my body, but also my mind.

I believed if I fell asleep again, I would die in my sleep. I dozed in and out until I had to get ready for work. I called the doctor, and during my appointment she suggested anti-depressants and seeing a therapist. She informed me that because of what was going on in my life I was, in fact, having anxiety attacks.

I tried to go back to my apartment to live, but I was still having a hard time. I ended up spending most of my time at my mother's home because I was afraid to go to sleep alone. I was afraid to drive by myself because I thought I was going to have an accident. I was afraid of everything and everybody. I suffered from insomnia and headaches. I could only sleep for two-hour periods. It didn't matter how late I stayed up at night, I could only sleep for two hours. There were times that I couldn't see; it was like I was going blind. My new life was almost as bad as my life in the emotionally abusive marriage.

One day I was driving down the street, tears rolled down my face as I listened to the radio. Still asking God why? Why allow me to stay in a marriage that was going to end in divorce? Why give me permission to leave the marriage and allow anxiety to attack me? WHY? As I drove, interrogating God, a song that came on the radio that gave me some clarity and ministered to my spirit. I can still hear gospel artist, LaShun Pace, singing the main line and the title of the song so powerfully, "For my Good, but For His Glory." I tapped in to my mustard seed faith.

I had been listening to Bishop T. D. Jakes and visiting the Potters House Dallas. On one visit, as he preached the Word of God, my faith began to strengthen. Shortly after I began attending regularly, First Lady, Serita Jakes, introduced "*God's Leading Ladies*" and a Life Enrichment Program for women called, "***Coming Out of The Shadows and into the Light. Coming from Behind the Curtain.***" I was hiding behind the curtain. I was scared. I was in an uncomfortable place and my life was in a mess. There were only a few days left to register for the class, and I didn't have the money.

One Sunday as they were announcing the registration deadline, a young lady sitting next to me said she wanted to attend but didn't have the money. I told her I was in the same position. Talk about fearless faith, we touched and agreed that day that both of us would be able to go. God answered our prayer. She received a scholarship from the First Lady. I still didn't know how I was going to go, but I trusted God

I was at work one day and I received a call from my sister-in-law that God told her to pay for me to go to "God's Leading Ladies." When she gave me the news the little girl in me cried like a baby. The program transformed my complete person. My life changed and through my pain, I found my purpose.

Bishop Jakes ministered a message called "The Frustration of Liberation." That message met me right where I was. My tears streamed like a water fountain as those words penetrated. I went home and bawled for days. God told me to write a letter to my husband requesting his forgiveness because although I may not have done what he did, I wasn't perfect. I also had a part in the downfall of our marriage. I was in disbelief. I was like, really God? You want me to do what? I knew the consequences of walking in disobedience, so I did exactly as I was instructed.

God brought me out of the bondage of my emotionally abusive marriage. During the time I was going through my painful marriage, God called me to preach. He didn't tell me, however, all that I would have to go through before allowing me to stand before his people.

On Sunday, September 29, 2013 I preached my first sermon, "**I'm On an Assignment**," taken from Jeremiah 29:11. I received my license to preach the Gospel that same day and am now an Ordained Minister. To God Be the Glory for all the good things He has done.

You have been fearfully and wonderfully made of God (Psalms 139:14). I pray that you are experiencing the blessings and walking in the favor of God during this season of your life. I am truly humbled and grateful to be walking in fearless faith and favor. That doesn't mean that life is perfect or that everything is where I want it to be. I have learned to lean and depend on God, no matter what's going on my life. Do I still get off track sometimes? Yes, I do. That's what keeps me humbled. I realize that I'm nothing without God and if He doesn't do it in me and through me, I cannot do it without Him. It's in Him that I live, move and have my being. (Acts 17:28)

My fearless faith was birthed out of struggle, heartaches, disappointments, bad decisions and pain. But, FEARLESS FAITH – which can come at a very high price – sustained me through all of that which I had gone through. My prayer is that it will do the same for you.

Building Your Fearless Faith Muscle:

1. Whatever situation you may find yourself in, fearless faith will allow you to experience God's grace and mercy like never before.

2. Trust and believe that God loves you and he knows what's best for you. He created you with a purpose, and he has a plan for your life.

3. He's not going to put more on you than you are able to bear because when it's time to bear it, he will supply exactly what you need.

4. Stand on the word of God. The devil may knock you down, but your fearless faith in God will pick you up. Be reminded that "though he slay me, yet will I trust him" (Job 13:15).

5. Keep your eyes lifted toward the hills from whence cometh your help; your help comes from the Lord (Psalms 121).

6. When he has tried you, you shall come forth as pure gold (Job 23:10). Stop focusing on where you are, or what you've been through and begin preparing yourself for where God is taking you.

In the words of Pastor T. L. Thompson, "THE BEST IS YET TO COME!"

CHAPTER 6
ANGELIQUE BROWN

Go Through It to Get to It

"Train up a child in the way he should go, when he is old he will not turn from it."
Proverbs 22:6

I grew up in a Baptist church; my grandfather was the pastor. I remember getting up on Sunday mornings, putting on pretty dresses, then sitting in church, eating peppermints and trying not to get caught falling asleep. So, I guess you could say I was "born into" putting God first and keeping His commandments. It was instilled in me from a young age that there was something bigger than myself. I also knew that like taking a breath, I was to thank and praise God for everything. The older I got; though, I noticed very few people in the church, including my family, practiced what they preached.

My mom taught me Bible stories and said prayers with me before bed; and she even bought me a tape of children's Bible songs with a little book to read and sing along. The songs taught me about the Lord's love in a way I could understand at a young age, and that me praying was a way of talking to Him. I could talk to him about anything. My grandmother always told me to pray - no matter what. She had a humble heart and spirit (except occasionally - about once a year – she'd slip a curse word out and all the kids would laugh). She showed us you don't always have to be perfect to love and be favored by the Lord. Without her, I would have rarely seen a true example of Christ at that stage in my life. Outside of my grandmother's house, there wasn't much holiness to see or hear.

I had a good childhood. I was loved by both parents and by all my family. Looking back, I know for sure at a young age Christ was in my heart. I obeyed my mother and my grandmother, Betty. They told to wear stockings and slips under my dress, close my legs and sit up straight. I did that. Ladies weren't supposed to slouch or sit with their legs open. Made sure not to do either. They taught me not to be around men without an equal number of women present and that I couldn't be where there were only men in the room - in any setting. I never learned how to play cards or dominoes because of this. Now I know they were trying to protect me; and now I see and understand why, so I am thankful they did.

<hr>

"For he shall give his angels charge over thee, to keep thee in all thy ways."
Psalms 91:11 (KJV)

My Gran-Gran, Betty, passed away in 2005. She was the backbone of the family, and I knew it wouldn't be easy on any of us. I had to remain strong for my mom. It was just her and me at the hospital most of the time; and we were there when Gran-Gran took her last breath. We asked the Lord to take her in peace and receive her with open arms. As we prayed, the room lit up where the wall and ceiling met at the foot of her bed. They were like small bright beams of light dancing on the ceiling.

I tapped my mom and asked, "Did you see that?" She nodded and simply said, "Yeah." Chills went through my body. I knew God was in that room; there was a peace that I'd never experienced. I remember my mom on one side of the bed and me on the other. My mom was holding Gran-Gran's right hand as I held her left hand. We held each other's hand in the middle. She squeezed my hand one last time and exhaled her last breath. As quickly as they came, the small beams of light went out the window. The gray overcast sky literally opened, a light shined down upon Seattle, and a group of seagulls circled in that light. I knew God had me there to witness what had happened in that room to strengthen me for my future and my purpose. I know my grandmother intentionally chose me to be there when she went home. I knew that day that if nothing else, I had a guardian angel for the rest of my life and God is more than real.

If there was any example of a woman of God in my world it was she. My Gran-Gran did right by every person encountered. She took people in when they had no place to go. She accepted two children in her life - born by her husband's lovers during her marriage. She kept the family together in love, no matter what. She taught me how to forgive and love unconditionally.

Isaiah 66:9 - "In the same way, I will not cause pain without allowing something new to be born"

The summer of 2006, my high school sweetheart and I would spend every Friday together and then spend Saturdays with other friends. One Friday, while we were split up, he went out with his friends and ended up getting into a wreck. The car went off a ramp and crashed in a ditch. I woke up the next morning to Myspace statuses saying, "Pray for MP," "Get well soon," "You're in my prayers," etc. My heart dropped. I was so scared another person I loved was going to leave me. I had never felt pain like that in my life. It was a different kind of worry because he wasn't old yet – I thought to myself - it wasn't "time" for him to go.

I went to the hospital. I had no idea how I got there - if I drove myself or if someone dropped me off. I vaguely remember walking through the hallway to the room where he was and seeing faces of friends and family crying. I went into his room and immediately began to pray over his body. After leaving the room, I went into a state of shock. I wasn't able to recognize him from the swelling in his head and face. I wanted to collapse. I found myself; again, being strong and praying over someone I loved who was about to pass away. And just like Gran-Gran, he passed soon after. I went numb and seemingly left my body. I don't even remember the moments after, making it home or the next few days.

This circumstance changed my life. It made me ask God, "Where are you in all this? How could you let a young man with a bright future die, just like that?" Talking to God and people who loved me got me through that hard time. His concern for me, and His encouragement through the words of others eased the pain of the circumstance. The more I prayed, and realized God was present, I realized I was never alone. By faith – God would strengthen and hold me. Although I, as well as the people closest to my boyfriend, couldn't see it at the time, his passing made us want to be better and do better. People who may not have done things to better themselves, in memory of him, decided to make some positive changes and that was a blessing. It may take days, months, or years to see what God is doing when travesty strikes in your life. But trust me, a blessing comes from EVERYTHING!

❧ —— ☙

"I have told you these things, so that in me you may have peace. In this world, you will have trouble. But take heart! I have overcome the world."

John 16:33 (KJV)

I kept to myself for a while after the death, until my best friend at the time begged me to get out the house. She wanted me to meet a guy who was a friend of the guy she was dating. After declining a few times, I gave in and went on a double date. That man, (whom I had no intentions of seeing again after a horrible date at Cheesecake Factory) quickly became the love of my life. He then became my husband and the father of our amazing daughter. The first year, I was the happiest woman alive. I had a great husband and not a worry in the world. As newlyweds, we had a lot of good times. We didn't have a wedding; instead, we went to a chapel with some friends as witnesses. We didn't even tell our parents or family for a while either and I never changed my last name. We feared they would be against the marriage and try to stop it from happening. I believe this tainted our marriage. No one knew. Other than my ring, there was no visible proof I was married. My love for him made none of that matter in the beginning, but I truly believe it all played a part in the marriage failing. As much as I hate to say it - the happiness was short lived. Seven months into the marriage, I became pregnant. Three months after becoming a new mother I started to feel things shift. Something in my spirit felt unsure about my husband. I took the matter to God. I prayed for God to show me what was causing me to feel this way and left it in His hands. That week, my husband was getting ready to leave on deployment for 10 months. I was going to be a new mother alone for the first time, with an unsettling feeling in my spirit. It was an anxiety that wouldn't go away. Less than a week before he left, God revealed to me that he was unfaithful. My entire world crashed. It was like everything around me was a lie. It was like one of those movies when you see land that is green and full of life then a shadow of darkness comes and overtakes the land, leaving it dead.

I snapped and confronted him. The neighbors heard my pain loud and clear that evening. But, I kept in mind that I asked God to show me. And He did! So, what now? My life felt like it was over. I was embarrassed; the person I vowed my life to had broken my heart I'd given him a child, and he didn't even respect that. I went into a deep depression. I called my cousins (who were like my sisters) and asked if my daughter and I could come stay with them. I needed help with this new baby who I couldn't get to eat or stop crying. I was in such a dark place. I needed to be around family.

Coping with being a new parent, separated from my husband while he was deployed, not understanding what I did wrong as a wife for him to do this, and not being able to discuss it face to face for months, had me in the fetal position crying myself to sleep most nights. I prayed for strength, but the devil got in my mind telling me all the things I was already thinking to keep me down. I wondered if it was because I didn't cook every day, or if he wasn't attracted to me anymore because I had a baby, did I let myself go or something, even thinking was I not thick enough? The devil answered yes to all of that. This started the season where I wanted him to feel what I felt and by doing what they call "looking for love in all the wrong places." I was hurt in a way I had never been before. The pain and anger got the best of me and I wanted it gone! I was young, and it didn't occur to me to give my pain, my will and my decisions to God. I regretted it every time. I kept telling myself I wasn't hurt when I was completely broken. At one point, I lost twenty pounds, my hair fell out, and I increased the partying and drinking to avoid everything that hurt.

I didn't understand how God would allow me to marry this man and have his child the "right way" and be so happy only to put me through all of this. I felt like what was the point of doing things right if life would still end up wrong. I put my faith on the back burner and lived out of character more than I ever had. Finding out about my husband's adultery created a sense of not caring about what I did for quite some time. I was attempting to fill the pain with the attention of other men. I stopped when I realized that it was leaving me empty and feeling worse. Truth be told, it was easier to question God than to point my finger at myself.

When my husband returned from his deployment, we talked things through and forgave each other. We tried to move forward for our family. We got orders to relocate and moved to Mississippi. We weren't there very long before we realized the trust was completely gone and things hadn't changed between or within us. Things got heated one night because we were living in the same house, but "not together." He looked through my phone and lost it over a text message. He started yelling in front of our daughter, who was two at the time. I tried to remain calm and assure her that it was okay. I begged for him not to behave like that in front of her. I grabbed her and tried to get in the car and leave. I put her in the car seat, but by the time I was getting in the driver seat he grabbed my arm and threw me unto the concrete. He took the keys and grabbed our daughter from the back seat as she was crying for me. I ran back into the house after them. I called my mom and told her what was going on; she called the police. Thank God, he put her down after she started screaming for me. When he did, she ran to me, and I ran to the kitchen with her in my arms. I grabbed a knife to defend us as I watched him with his fists balled up like he was going to punch me.

I had to stay with my daughter in that house with a knife pretty much scared for our lives because I had never seen this side of him and didn't know what to expect until police arrived. The police escorted my daughter and me to a shelter because we had nowhere else to go. It was the most embarrassing and degrading situation I had ever experienced. I just kept smiling at my baby telling her everything was okay, and I loved her. I had to fill out papers and learn the shelter's rules. I finally went to bed at two o'clock in the morning. I didn't sleep though; I laid there holding my daughter, looking at the environment and seeing all these other women with their children that had lived there for months. As soon as the sun rose I started making phone calls, praying, "Lord, please get us out of here."

I was supposed to stay a few days to make reports but after I talked to my cousin, she bought us Greyhound tickets to Savannah, Georgia, which was the closest place we could go. I then called the one person I befriended while I was there and asked her to pick us up. I snuck out the shelter with my daughter and was gone. With pistol in hand, my friend took me home so I could grab some things.

She told my husband, hand on her gun, "The police know we're here. She's packing a bag and if you try anything I will have to shoot you."

He kissed his daughter goodbye and she dropped us off at the bus station. We rode a Greyhound for about six hours to Georgia and stayed there with my cousin for a few months. During this time, I wasn't hurting for myself but the fact that my daughter had to witness and go through something so young bothered me. I could only pray she would forget it.

Sadly, after a long break apart, the vicious cycle began of me leaving my husband and coming back. Each time I foolishly thought the time away had healed all and things would change. They got worse each time. Each time there were more people we brought into the madness. Each time we separated we gained more soul ties by dating other people, never having resolved the issues between us. Nothing we were doing apart or together was blessed.

Neither of us took our marriage seriously. We didn't even legally divorce before moving on to new relationships. After I realized I wasn't feeling better by dating other men, I stopped dating. I did what most Christians do when they go against God's direction for their life – I ran back to God begging for forgiveness. I wanted to be back in God's good graces. I wanted to try to work it out with my husband. I depended on God to rescue me because I knew He would never leave nor forsake me - even in my ignorance.

Family and friends encouraged me to work on my marriage for my daughter's sake. Family members would say, "You won't have to struggle." Man, were they wrong! The marriage was a constant struggle. Every time I moved out and tried to make it on my own, I struggled. I found it hard to get my own life together. I felt like my family wanted me to deal with the trust issues and cheating going on in my marriage than to help me through my struggle. I knew that I would rather have peace in an uncomfortable situation than to try and be comfortable in confusion.

During my hardest moments when I didn't have anyone to talk to about my marriage - without being judged - I had to talk to God and pray for strength, guidance and forgiveness. That's how I managed to keep peace for my daughter and me on the rollercoaster that had become our life. Up and down, round and round, the rollercoaster ride seemed as if it would never end. Sadly, I would pray for guidance; God would guide me away. Yet, I would go back, hoping my husband would be different. I guess you could say I was hard headed. I should have ended it, but I had to keep going through it until I got tired of learning that lesson. Sometimes God will keep letting you go through things until you get the lesson. Sometimes your suffering is on you.

There were times where I would be good; usually when I was single, had a good job and could manage things. Then I'd get into a relationship thinking I could love again, thinking I healed myself and God would honor that mess. And, because I was still legally married, how in the world did I think any other relationship was going to work? My life continued to get harder. Just because we were separated did not give us the okay to date - at least not date and it be blessed. I had to sit in my foolishness. I knew what we were doing was wrong. My mentality was, "Well, he cheated on me first, so I can do whatever I want." Yeah, right! That was the hardheaded side of me rearing its ugly head again. There was the little devil on one shoulder telling me it was okay to keep dating other people, even while in my marriage. Clearly, I had knocked God off the other shoulder because I took the enemy's advice and continued to date against God's will. Fail, fail, and fail. After my last failed relationship, God told me to be single and get myself together; get closer to Him, fully heal and let Him bless me. I told myself I would no longer give a man more attention than the Lord, so I tried to distance myself from men and dating.

*"But their scribes and Pharisees murmured against his disciples, saying, why do ye eat and drink with publicans and sinners? And Jesus answering said unto them, **they** that are whole need not a physician; but they that are sick. I came not to call the righteous, but sinners to repentance."*

Luke 5:31-32 (KJV)

I was living in Texas in 2017 and didn't know many people. Most of the people I knew would go out, so I would go along just so I wouldn't be at home bored and alone. During a night out, I saw a man that stood out to me. We exchanged numbers that night but ended up having a conversation before we left the parking lot. From the first conversation, he shared that he was celibate... and immediately God spoke to me and said, "That's what you need to do." I knew at that moment I was meant to meet him if only to hear those words and change my path forever. Although it was easier said than done, and I failed a few times before I succeeded, I continued on the path to celibacy. I knew I was tired of doing things my way and tired of being hurt in the process. Tired of my mind guiding my body. Tired of my body acting without consideration. Tired of not allowing my spirit to guide both my mind and body. I kept the faith. I believed God would honor my pursuit to be pure and please Him. I repented and distanced myself from the things that would put a wedge between God and me. With that knowledge and awareness guiding me, it made it easier not to enter lustful relationships or behaviors again.

I continued to seek God and become closer to Him in all that I did. I continued to seek God by reading my Bible and praying daily about everything. I went to church twice a week to stay in a state of learning about the spirit and to be surrounded by people on the same path as me. I didn't let my shortcomings be the end. I asked God to give me more strength and wisdom to not let lust overcome me and to live purer. I then made a vow before God to be celibate until I remarried and to give Him more time than anyone or anything else in my life. As I kept my vow, God continued to show me that I would be blessed, and my purpose would be revealed.

I cried out to God and asked Him to show me the crooked places within me and for Him to make them straight. I asked Him to help me remove everything in me that displeased Him. I prayed to be cleansed and for Him to use me for His purpose. Never before had I asked God for these things myself. I figured He knew what was wrong in me and would help me get past it. I fasted, for the second time in my life, for seven days. I needed to hear a word from God to keep me going and to be strong on my celibacy journey. I needed Him to guide me to my purpose. In more than one way, He spoke to me regarding all those things. I felt connected more than ever and felt that my storm was almost over. There are still moments when things in my life are out of my hands, and I don't know what's going to happen. But, I've learned to exercise fearless faith knowing that I am in God's hands. I trust the outcome in His will, in His perfect plan, and I will survive.

"For this is the love of God, that we keep his commandments: and his commandments are not grievous."

1 John 5:3 (KJV)

Looking back at my life, I can see God has never left me. No matter how messed up I was - or thought I was – He was there, and there was always a lesson in everything. God wanted me to love Him and put my full trust in Him as much I gave love and trust to the wrong men. God wanted me to know that only He could heal me of my hidden hurts. It took a lot of let downs to get to the point where I finally and truly heard what God was saying to me. I couldn't keep straddling the fence and expect to receive the good He has planned for me. I am not perfect - nor will I ever be - but I will continue to pursue being more like Christ.

❧———☙

"A new heart also will I give you, and a new spirit will I put within you: and I will take away the stony heart out of your flesh, and I will give you and heart of flesh. And I will put my spirit within you, and cause you to walk in my statutes, and ye shall keep my judgments, and do them."

Ezekiel 36:26-27 (KJV)

My faith began to perfect once I fully gave myself to God, strived to be purer and stayed in His presence every day. In this new space that I'm in, I avoid lust and my former sin-sick nature so that I am blessed beyond my biggest dreams. For a long time, I've had compassion and empathy for other women and young women who are going through bad relationships/marriages, abuse, cheating, lack of confidence struggles, because I've been through it. I know without God I wouldn't have gotten through any of it. I encourage them and help them to grow closer to God and avoid the mistakes I've made. I felt as if I wasn't good enough and God couldn't use me. I knew if I got the chance, I would change the path of someone's life, so they could experience this fearless faith.

God has shown me more than once in dreams that I would have a platform to speak to thousands of women and encourage them through my story and my faith. I didn't know how or when this would come to fruition but I knew the whole list of my woes: failed marriage, wrong relationships, distance from God, not having a job, almost being homeless, staying in a shelter with my two-year-old, sleeping on family members couches, working and trying to save money to get on my feet, trying to go back to school only to have the dream snatched from under me, and living in six different states, was all for a reason. All of these things gave me compassion, empathy, understanding, patience and love for people. I admit, some things I did to myself, but others were intentionally planned to be my downfall. He heard my many prayers over the years. He searched my heart and brought me to this moment of obedience to show me my God-given purpose is coming to fruition effectively immediately.

∞—∞

"And all these blessings shall come on thee, and overtake thee, if thou shalt hearken unto the voice of the LORD thy God."

My storm was drawn out for nine years. I often wondered when it would be over? When would I just have a break from struggle, hurt and disappointment? I had to go through it to get to it — "it" being my place of peace. I always knew Christ was within me even when I wanted to lose faith. I wanted to lose faith when I didn't have all the answers and I thought I needed them. Now I know I didn't need to have all the answers; that's what faith in God is for and about. You are not alone; and the battle isn't just yours. If you can't do it alone, bring it to God, and leave it there with Him; have faith - what is His will for you will be done.

Deuteronomy 28:2 (KJV)

I thought about the times I could've been homeless, and I wasn't, the times I could've died but I didn't. God blessed me with a child full of love, intelligence and understanding. To her, everything was just another adventure, and if I said things were okay, she believed me and in me. During my darkest moments, my faith was near and kept me; for it was all a part of God's plan for me. None of the trials lasted forever. Sometimes He needed me closer to Him. When you are so low all you can do is look up and realize He is with you, you draw closer to Him. I smile and thank Him for the unseen battles He fought for me. I thank Him because unless you were there you wouldn't know what I've been through by looking at me or watching my life from the outside. I have had a lot of good days, which far outweigh my bad days; but it's those bad days that built my character. It's that humbleness from my experiences that brought me to my testimony. If all I had were good days, then what would I write about? How would I be able to encourage and uplift other women's lives?

God hand-picked me to go through hard times but never let me completely lose my faith; nor did He leave me in hard times or faltering faith. He never let me walk completely off the edge. He kept me uncomfortable enough to learn my lessons. I am here because I never gave up I prayed in the lowest moments and I thanked Him in the hardest times.

View everything in your life as a lesson or a blessing. When things are good, or when things are bad, have fearless faith that the Lord is with you always. He will never leave you. What you're going through has a purpose bigger than yourself. Continue to pray and thank Him through it all because your testimony is on the way!!

Building Your Fearless Faith Muscle:

1. Before you do anything, ask yourself if God is in it.

2. View everything as either a blessing or a lesson.

3. Pray and thank God for the good and the bad, the yes and the no.

4. Believe EVERYTHING is for a greater good. It all has purpose.

5. If you feel like all else has failed, pray and rest.

When God Says Yes

"For I know the thoughts that I think toward you, says the LORD, thoughts of peace and not of evil, to give you a future and a hope."

Jeremiah 29:11

Have you ever had your soul emptied out? Have you ever cried out in the dead of night to darkness so deep that you were sure death was a better alternative than the life you were living? I have. I have persevered through some difficult times. I have made some good and bad decisions and I own them all. Like many women, I created a plan for my life and I pursued it with everything in me with little thought of God. I was forced to learn to walk through the consequences of giving little thought to the one who keeps me in mind.

In 1996, I made the decision to get married; despite the signs that this was not the best decision for me. I did not do the things that the Bible prescribed for marriage. I put my husband in the place of God in my life. I lived with him before we got married. I indulged in using marijuana and alcohol daily. I cussed and fought with him. I worshipped our money and our material possessions. I lived the lifestyle I wanted to live. I shopped when I wanted to. I traveled when I wanted to. I did whatever I wanted to do. I had it going on. So, I thought. I felt like nothing could touch us. I was full of pride. Because of doing it my way I suffered the consequences. My son suffered. We all suffered. Divorce became the only solution. But, after the divorce I was broken hearted and empty. I did not recognize myself. I could not believe the person I had become. I was so far from myself that some days I did not know how I would make it.

When my plans did not work out - I realized I needed God. I had put my trust in people. The Bible says to put your trust in the Lord. That was lesson number one. I learned to trust in the Lord after putting my trust in a man, in my finances, in my education and in everything else. By the time I finally realized the Lord was the only one I could trust I had built up so many idols that I would spend several years tearing them down.

There I was, a broken single mother of a young son whom I never planned to raise by myself. I was reduced to the narrative told so many times in the black community of another single black woman raising a young black boy without a father in the home. The shame of having failed in my marriage was overwhelming. The guilt I felt for not being able to keep my family together was crippling. Not to mention the devastating effects of the divorce on my son. He witnessed the fighting and the arguing. He carried the weight of it all as a child. It was so unfair for him to be put in the middle of adult mess. Yet there he was. Even today he suffers from the pain of the immaturity I displayed in front of him. It was damaging to his self-esteem. He is still recovering today from having his family destroyed. God had mercy on me and He delivered me from that marriage in 2003 but not before teaching me valuable lessons. For that, I am grateful.

There was no longer anyone else for me to blame for my life. I had to pick up the pieces and figure out how to put my life back together. I could no longer look to my husband and say that he was responsible for my life. I had to own the fact that I did not like the person that I had become. I was not living the life in private that I projected publicly. I had to admit that I was wearing a mask. I had hidden skeletons in my closet that were there each day to haunt me and remind me of my devastating loss. I was extremely disappointed in myself for this failure. I played the circumstances of my life over and over in my mind like a movie. I was searching for the point where things had gone wrong. I could not find the answer as so many things flooded each scene. They had all played a part in the destruction, so it was useless to try to pinpoint one thing. What I knew was that everything that I had built my life around was now demolished. The family unit was gone. Our home was gone. I had no money and I was broke. More importantly I was broken. There was confusion and chaos in my life that I had let in. I had to sit in that reality, and it was a devastating reality. I needed my mind renewed and Jesus was the only one who could do that. At this point God had my full attention.

In 2003, I made the decision to continue my studies and pursue a doctoral degree. Earning my doctoral degree provided a distraction from the piercing pain and overwhelming loss that I felt every day after the divorce. There was no way I could finish my dissertation without God and remain sane with all that I had been through. As God showed me the blueprint for healing and renewing my mind He also showed me how to finish my dissertation. He increased my prayer life; and I started attending church regularly and studying the Bible. I attended Bible study on Wednesday nights and I learned more about His word. He put more mature women in my circle that told me the truth and challenged my thinking. These women taught me how to pray and then prayed with me to help strengthen my faith.

The Holy Spirit revealed that I was woefully ignorant about men and relationships. I had not had a strong relationship with my father growing up. Most women learn how to interact with men through that first relationship with their father. I trusted what God was telling me; and I surrendered myself to His understanding and growing in the knowledge of the subject. God consistently placed people around me to give me golden nuggets of knowledge on men and relationships. I completed the homework assignments in books to help me better examine and understand what I did not know. While I was researching my dissertation topic I was also learning more about how to have God-ordained relationships that would lead to a healthy marriage.

First, I had to learn to be alone. I had to learn that I was completely whole without a man. This was a new revelation. Every message I had received from the time I was a young girl indicated that I could not be whole without a man. The strength and discipline it took for me to find a place within me that was okay being alone was difficult yet empowering. Coming to terms with what my ignorance about men had cost me in my marriage was a humbling experience. The entire process developed me academically; and healed me emotionally. God helped me to see my strength through Him. He renewed my mind and strengthened my faith with every word I read and wrote. With God's grace and guidance, I finished my doctoral degree and graduated in 2010.

God continued to test me to mature and perfect my faith. I had it locked in my mind that I would receive a promotion in my career after finishing my doctorate. I was ready to begin the next phase of my career and I believed God was going to restore all that I had lost financially. I was certain that God had ordained a promotion with my name on it. When I prayed about it, the Holy Spirit said that it was not the right time for me to make a career move. I did not hear what I wanted to hear as a result of my prayers, so I decided what I heard was paralyzing fear trying to keep me from moving forward. I decided that I had worked hard, and I should go after my next goal with passion and determination. I completed multiple job applications and I went on numerous interviews with no success. I was completely frustrated, and I wasted months of my time walking in disobedience. I needed a better job, because I had a vision of home ownership in front of me. Still, God had to deal with me instead about my disobedience and impatience. It was completely crazy of me to try to override God's decision and plan for my life, yet I did. God said in Jeremiah 29:11 that He knows the plans that He has for my life. God speaks with the complete authority of being sovereign and omniscient. He knows the past, present and future of all His children. Clearly, I was still spiritually immature, and I had more to learn.

I submitted to God and put my focus back on Him and the dream of owning a place where my son and I could put down roots and work to re-establish our lives. We had lived in apartments since we were put out of our home by my ex-husband. I will never forget the feeling of utter betrayal when he announced we had thirty days to vacate our home. After weeks of searching, my young son and I found a one-bedroom apartment. The first night we moved in, we made a bed on the floor using blankets and a pile of clothes. My husband had refused to help me move any of the furniture from the home. I did not have any money to pay anyone to help me. It did not matter that we had no furniture. We had peace and quiet and that was more valuable than furniture. We were safe in our own space and that was what mattered most.

I was ready to build memories in a new home with my son. I wanted him to have a place where he could invite his friends over for sleepovers and parties. I wanted to entertain my friends and create a space that my son and I could both be proud of living in every day. I envisioned my son going away to college and coming back for the holidays and bringing friends to our home. I could already see the holiday decorations, the lights and warm embers of a fireplace burning as the years of happy memories unfolded as we spent the major holidays together. I wanted a place big enough so if any of my family members wanted to visit they would not have to stay in a hotel because there was enough space for them in my home. I also wanted to prove to myself that I could do this by myself. I would never let anyone put me in a position where my son and I did not have a place to live. I would never be that vulnerable again. I had now set a goal of home ownership that would challenge me to stand in my own strength and power as a competent and capable woman. There was nothing wrong with me feeling empowered, yet I needed to remember that God was in control. He would teach me along the way of this home buying experience.

In prior years, I was told I needed a substantial down payment which totaled thousands of dollars. I did not have thousands of dollars. My salary barely allowed me to meet my financial obligations. I am so thankful that in God's kingdom it is not about how much money we make. It is about how much faith we have in Him to do the thing that we are trusting in Him to do. As I looked at the situation it seemed impossible to achieve this dream or to even know where to start. I knew the rent I was paying at the time was as high as a mortgage. I was tired of giving my money away with no tax benefit or the opportunity to build equity and wealth. When a friend recommended a realtor, she had worked with to buy her home I figured I should at least give her a call. I knew enough through my graduate studies that if this was a goal I had better start the process as it might take years to accomplish. I took a deep breath and put aside my fears. I activated my faith and reached out to the realtor. One of the first things my realtor did was pray with me. God was working this situation out for my good. At the time I did not fully understand the amazing power of having a realtor who was a prayer warrior. I would come to appreciate this valuable asset much later in the process. Proverbs 27:17 says, "Iron sharpens iron, and one man sharpens another." Her prayers with and for me helped me get through the ups and downs of the home buying process and strengthened my prayer life.

The next step in the process was to talk with a mortgage lender. Again, God stepped into this process and my realtor directed me to her mortgage lender to begin the financing process. I remember being very afraid to make that initial call. It was in financial matters where I had the least confidence. As I braced myself for the worst I hesitantly picked up the phone and slowly dialed the numbers. One ring, two rings, three rings and the greeting came on inviting me to leave a message. I was relieved. The lender immediately called me back. We talked for a while and she reassured me that if I would decide to entrust her with my mortgage needs, that she would work with me to find the right mortgage product. That conversation reminded me to not let anyone discourage me from my dreams. With God there is always a way to accomplish what we desire. It may take a little time, but God will put the right people in our path to help us to get us there.

By faith I began to gather the necessary documents the lender requested, and I gave her access to my credit report. God showed up again as it turned out that my credit score was not as bad as I thought. It had been more than seven years since I'd declared bankruptcy and I had paid bills on time and resisted the temptation to incur debt through credit cards, which repaired my credit. It was high enough for me to qualify for a mortgage loan. We always imagine in our minds a much worse scenario than our reality even though God tells us in His word in Proverbs 3:5 to trust in the Lord with all our heart and lean not to our own understanding. I have learned that these are not just words written in the Bible. They are promises meant to guide our daily lives and our journey to His abundance and to the desires in our heart. I have no doubt that God was working with my lender as she worked with me.

This was an exciting time as I watched God work. I began praying every day and I thanked God in advance for my home. When I fully surrendered my heart to God, I began to rest in the peace of knowing that He was in control. Yes, there were times when my faith got weak and I had to literally cry out to God in prayer. I was thankful for all those lessons on how to pray that mentors and spiritual advisors had given me. Even in those times that my faith wavered I knew He was going to do something amazing during this process. I was committed to not settling for something less than God's best for me. I had done that in so many areas in my life in the past. That had cost me in the end and I was not going to make that mistake again.

My realtor took me to see several properties that were fixer uppers within my price range, but none of them appealed to me. I resisted the urge to settle. I had lived in a fixer-upper before and I promised myself that I would never do that again. I was interested in a newer home and I had already decided on the neighborhood. The home prices in my desired neighborhood were much higher than what I qualified for. I drove through my desired neighborhood and I went in to tour the model home. I had read that it was important for me to have a vision for my dreams. Getting a vision for the home that God could possibly bless me with filled me with joy. I began dreaming of what it would be like to pull into the neighborhood each day and ride past the lake with the beautiful waterfall. I could see myself taking a brisk run, a long walk, or a bike ride through the scenic trails throughout the neighborhood. I sat for a moment and enjoyed the peaceful and serene environment. I could see my son making new friends and playing in the neighborhood. I already saw us living there. It was simply a matter of God intervening on our behalf to make this dream a reality.

After I prayed about it I reached out to my realtor to ask her to pull a list of available properties in the neighborhood. This time I heard a yes in my spirit when I prayed even though all the financial evidence said no. She reminded me of my qualification amount and shared that these homes were out of my reach. I explained to her that I understood, yet, I still wanted to see homes in the neighborhood. I told her I was putting my trust in God to deliver on His promise of yes. To my realtor's surprise she was able to find two properties within my price range in the neighborhood. We set up a time to visit the two houses. While both homes were in the neighborhood neither was what I desired. They were not God's best for me and I was not going to settle. The next property had people still living in it.

The Holy Spirit prompted me to ask my realtor to take a drive around to the back of the neighborhood. It was then that we saw the sign in the yard to my house. We wrote down the address and I asked my realtor to pull that listing. This looked more like the kind of property I would be interested in living in with my son. She pulled the listing and set up an appointment for us to see the property. This visit was much different than the others. It was as if God Himself showed up and entered the property before us. I was warmly greeted by the homeowner and given a tour of the home. The homeowner explained that he was in the military and he and his wife were moving due to a new assignment. The home was in pristine condition. It was beautifully decorated using a Feng shui design. I was more and more impressed as I walked through each room.

Praying and listening to the Spirit as I walked through this home I kept hearing a yes in my spirit. Everything about this home from the fireplace to the finished basement to the paint on the walls was exactly what I had dreamed of. God had already given me a vision of living in this home. It was a done deal as far as I was concerned. To confirm God's hand and His favor during that visit the homeowner expressed to me that he wanted me to have the house. He shared that he felt I should have it and he was going to do what he could to ensure that I was able to purchase this home for me and my son. That was God speaking and I knew it. He explained that he had some room to negotiate the price of the house due to the housing market instability. He knew he would receive some assistance from the military as they needed to move quickly and that should supplement any gaps between what I qualified for and the actual price of the house. In that one conversation it was clear to me that God's favor had already intervened on my behalf. It was as finished as Jesus hanging on the cross; we just had to go through the process.

I want you to understand how magnificent our God is. The price of the home was one hundred and twenty-five thousand dollars over what I had qualified for. I knew God would have to intervene for me to afford this house. With His whisper of yes in my spirit, I asked my realtor to put a contract on the house. I activated my faith. She wrote the contract and made the offer to the seller. He immediately accepted the offer. I did not have a down payment or closing costs. Nor did I have the earnest money deposit that was needed to show that I was a serious buyer once the contract was accepted. I was truly walking by faith. Who buys a house with no money except someone with fearless faith? God was not finished teaching me lessons.

Soon after I put the contract on the house I learned that my position at my school had been downsized and my salary had been significantly cut, leaving me wondering if this was the best time for me to even think about trying to purchase a home. I was devastated and frustrated all at the same time. Not only was I not receiving a promotion, I was going to be making even less money than before. Not exactly what I was hoping for but an exact recipe for God to work a miracle. I cried out to God asking why He would let me get my hopes up about this house only to have my dreams dashed once again. I mean what kind of God does that to His children? I was ready to give up. I was tired; and I could feel that brokenness coming upon me once again that I had felt before. I was ready to bow out and then God showed up.

My lender called to tell me she had done further research on home buying programs that fit my circumstances. She had found a program for middle income home buyers that would assist with down payment and closing costs. The decrease in my salary put me below the income requirement by seventy-five dollars and I now qualified for a ten thousand dollar grant to cover the down payment and closing costs. This grant was money that I would never have to pay back. You know I was shouting, right? Only when we put our lives in God's capable hands can we witness Him work a miracle. He is the only one who can decrease and increase us at the same time.

God had provided the down payment and now the closing costs were covered. I knew He would also provide that earnest money deposit my realtor was waiting for. When God spoke to my spirit and asked me to seek help from others I knew He was doing something special in me. It was another lesson. I have always been very determined and independent. I like to help people and it is very hard for me to be on the end of needing help. To this day I still have a hard time asking people for help and I continue to work on it. I obeyed God when He told me to call my mother, my sister and a friend and ask for the money needed. This was such a humbling experience because I had to admit that I do not always have it all together. God was breaking me and delivering me from a heart full of pride and that independent spirit. When I asked each of them they were eager to help. They each gifted me five hundred dollars toward the purchase of the house. The lesson for me was to allow God to use people to bless me. It is not always about me. Sometimes it is about God getting a blessing to others by allowing them to help me. I received that lesson.

The contract negotiations between the seller's military benefits and the bank took about six months as the price I offered fell significantly short of the initial value of the house. I rested in God's promise that it was going to happen. The day I received the call from my lender that our closing date was two weeks away exhilarated me. It had been a long journey and there was one more lesson. My mortgage lender asked me for three months of bank statements. During the months of negotiations, I had to adjust to the cut in my salary and my bank statements reflected negative balances in my account on several occasions. I was horrified as I believed this would damage my chances to finalize the loan as it still had to go to the mortgage underwriter. Once again God intervened. After reviewing the bank statements, my lender reached out to me and before I could say anything she shared that she was going to write a letter on my behalf. Her letter would advocate for me with the underwriter. The underwriter accepted her confidence in me and my loan was approved. God and I had won.

On January 25, 2011, we went to closing on our home. We moved in that same day shouting and praising God for the excellent things He had done. God had walked me out of darkness into His marvelous light. From the divorce, through finishing school, to buying this home He had developed my fearless faith in Him. I wish I could report that everyone was happy about the process that God took me through and that everyone who began the journey with me was with me in the end. I had to leave some people behind who I considered friends as they could not fully appreciate the way God had transformed my life and my circumstances. I have learned to be okay with that. It was a difficult journey and I would not change one part of it.

Now I know that when God says yes, it is yes. It does not matter what circumstances I must grow through to get to that yes. I am sure that whatever it is that He promised me it will come to pass. I do not take my eyes off God. I continue to trust His word and I delight myself in Him. I let Him work things out in my life. Yes, I get weary along the way and I may waver in my faith, but I come right back to the lessons He taught me in some of the darkest times in my life. I have His word hidden in my heart. In 2017, my son and I had a big party to celebrate our seventh year in our home. I am clear that this house is ours because I lived out the fearless faith written in the words in Matthew 9, "according to your faith let it be done to you;" and in Hebrews 11:1, *"Now faith is the substance of things hoped for, the evidence of things not seen."*

Building Your Fearless Faith Muscle:

1. Stay Connected and Trust God to Handle His Business - God is sovereign. He does not need our help with anything He is doing. Let Him handle

what belongs to Him. Seek Him to know what belongs to us and focus on doing what He gives us to do.

2. Stop Thinking About It, Start Praying About It - Our thinking can get us in trouble. We think from a logical and rational perspective. Sometimes God's way is not rational or logical. Through prayer, we can get peace about a situation and develop the patience to wait on God and His timing.

3. Partner with Others and Ask for Help - People and relationships are our most valuable assets. Take no one for granted and look for the strengths in each person. They are always there even when they are hard to find. Appreciate and admire the differences in others. Learn from others and build a winning team of supporters. When we bring our unique gifts and talents together, we accomplish the impossible.

The Greatest Love of All: Forgiveness

"I said in my heart, God shall judge the righteous and the wicked, for there is a time for every purpose and for every work."

Ecclesiastes. 3:17

Why wasn't it me? Honestly, that day he died, I died with him. My life taken right along with his. That gunshot penetrated his back and pierced my heart at the same time. His life, and my love… gone. I no longer felt safe. My protector, the one who kept me guarded, and unconditionally loved me, my baby brother was taken right before my eyes.

This is where it all began. Mych (my brother), a friend, and me were at a local gas station in my neighborhood. Anthony (someone who I was previously involved with) happened to drive by. He saw us and decided to turn around, for only God knows what, especially considering the fact that there was an order of restraint against me to not be within fifty feet of him. A slight altercation ensued. I told Anthony to leave Mych out of it, because the problem was between him and me. That was the end of that…or so I thought.

After that incident, I felt pressed to apologize to Anthony about what had transpired earlier that day at the gas station. I felt obligated because I saw how it was dragging other people into the chaos, and it was my duty since I had, years before, slashed his face with a razor blade. I called, he answered, and we talked and went over the events. Again, I apologized and expressed my regret for my actions, and how it wasn't my intent to harm him in such a way. By the end of the conversation, I believed my apology was accepted and we were moving on from it.

Weeks later, Mych and I were at home while our parents were away on a trip. He and I spent two weeks together, just the two of us. I believe God strategically orchestrated this. He knew that I needed this time with Mych because within the following two weeks, Mych would be gone in the physical form. All that would be left were the memories of him. God knows His plans, we don't, and so we can't see or understand the things that happen or that we grow through until after the fact. Mych and I barely did anything together during this time. I was working and going to school. He worked, and his day was full with his daughter. We were busy, but when we were done with our daily tasks, I would have to say that hanging out together at home was the crown of it all. Not that what we talked about was so significant, the honor was just being together. If I knew then that in a few weeks I would never see him again, I would have absolutely told him I loved him more than he would ever know, and that I was proud of him and enjoyed having him for my little brother. That I appreciated the unconditional love he always gave and showed me.

Easter fell during those two weeks and we went to church together. I was glad he went. During those days, my parents and I had begun to attend regularly, but him not so much. It was funny because during our time, I had been sharing the word with him. I'm not sure if it fell on deaf ears or not, but it just always seemed like he wasn't listening. The time was getting closer for our parents to return home. I remember one of the nights, Mych came in the house and it was kind of late. I'm not sure if it was noticeable to him, but I could feel that the energy had changed when he came into the house.

Normally the energy is light and comforting, but this time it was dark and gloomy. Next thing I knew, I heard the spirit of the Lord say, "You guys aren't going to be together long." Tears began to run down my face as sadness came over me. I'm sure he didn't see the tears, or he would have asked what was wrong, as he was so attentive to me like that. In that moment I felt those words, but I was clueless as to what they meant…until the day came that would change my family's life forever.

Much of it feels like a blur. I remember talking to Anthony and apologizing. The next thing I remember was being in the park with Mych. Within fifteen to twenty minutes of us being there, Anthony showed up. Some words were exchanged, then Mych was on the ground with a bullet in his back - all at the hands of Anthony, the person who I just asked to not bring my little brother into our issues; the person who was supposed to be like an older brother to Mych. The person who once had my heart and I loved dearly. That bullet eventually took my brother's life and I never saw it coming. I found myself kneeled down by Mych's right side begging him to ask God to forgive him of his wrong doings, and to accept Jesus as his Lord and savior. What a time to ask, right? During this time was he conscious? Yes, his eyes were moving back and forth, but he never said any words. I could see the pain in his face, and I kept hearing him gasping, as if the bullet was burning or hurting his insides. Everyone that was there stood around in disbelief as we waited for the paramedics to come.

Anthony came into my life when I was about fifteen years old. My goodness! What I wouldn't give to go back to that time. Back to that time when things weren't so hectic, chaotic and seemingly in shambles. Our paths crossed intentionally even before we were ever thought of. First because God knew us before he formed us in our mother's womb. Secondly, our mothers were friends in there adolescent years. TK and I met in middle school, which were our sixth to eighth grade years. Our paths crossed continuously over this time. Our friends dated each other, and we knew each other's name and face. We were never friends, though. Interesting enough, we end up at the same high school and then became a couple.

At first, being young, it was an innocent boyfriend and girlfriend thing. But as time passed and we grew older, and so did our feelings and emotions. Like any other relationship, we had our ups and downs, breakups and make-ups, and everything else in between. All I knew was Anthony was my friend, and sometimes this was how relationships could be. I didn't know that what we were experiencing was unhealthy. I know this now because of reading books that talk about emotional abuse, verbal abuse, mental abuse, and what these traits looked like.

After reading and having conversations with people who wanted our love to flourish, I realized both of us had growing to do. No one ever told me that communication was a big factor in making or breaking a relation-ship. Communication comes with so many components. The actual words spoken, the tone you use, and the non-verbal aspects as well. Being assertive, aggressive, passive-aggressive, being submissive and/or manipulative. All these methods can steer a conversation to its end. Along with getting my understanding, the revelation of this helped me to see that my experience steered me to communicate harshly at times. I was very aggressive to men and submissive to women. After high school, I decided to head to college. Life's lessons were still happening and teaching me about what life had to offer whether good or bad, winning or losing. What I didn't realize was that I wasn't paying attention; I was simply living day to day. When I woke up each morning, I wasn't thinking or planning to tackle specific tasks that were going to catapult me into the life I wanted.

So, the summer of 1999, I headed to college in Virginia. But it meant leaving Anthony. I had to do it for me. I was proud of myself. My future was looking like something good could be happening. I had no plan on what that was, but I knew it was something, so I stood by myself and moved forward, I never heard Anthony tell me he was proud of me, so I had to be for myself.

One night I went on a date, I really didn't know this person, or should I say, I didn't see him often. He wasn't a student at the school. He was what the students called a "local," meaning he was from the area. We met in a setting where I felt safe, but you never know people and their intent. We exchanged numbers and eventually got together. In all honesty, if I saw him today I wouldn't even know him. Since I wasn't from VA, as I told him, he said he wanted to show me around. I took him up on his offer. He picked me up one night, and as I got into the car he passed me a blunt he was smoking. This wasn't uncommon because we had met at a gathering at friend's house where I was smoking weed and he happened to partake as well. At that point in my life, I had been smoking weed for years so it wasn't like I was being forced to do this or that it was foreign to me. I took a couple of puffs, and if my memory serves me correctly, I may have had a few sips of alcohol. But after that, I DO NOT REMEMBER ANYTHING! I can't place what happened from the time I got in the car to the next. I don't know how much time had passed at that point, but I finally came to and was being carried into this dark house. Then I was out again. I have no idea how I got back into my dorm room, I assumed that by that time I had regained full consciousness.

My body didn't feel right. I knew he had taken advantage of me. I was so embarrassed. I didn't say anything. Was that his intention, to get me high and rape me? SICK. He then continued his assault by calling and harassing me, leaving creepy messages on my answering machine. I had told only one of my friends, who was so gracious and non-judgmental toward me about the whole situation She did all that she could to comfort me. I stewed in my embarrassment and shame. How did I let this happen? How could I be so stupid? Eventually my mind convinced me that I wasn't going to make it in school, so I left Virginia, and without finishing school.

The word says: *"the thief does not come except to steal, and to kill, and to destroy. I have come that they may have life, and that they may have it more abundantly. (John 10:10 NKJV).*

Looking back on the situation, I can see how this incident was a part of a setup - a chain of events to destroy my spirit and break me down. I put that situation out of my mind and buried it with the rest of the times I had been taken advantage of sexually. When I think about the pattern of sexual abuse I'd experienced in my life, I now recognize the cycle of abuse that kept me going back to Anthony. I sometimes wish I had recognized it sooner.

Moving back home was good for me at that point. I continued chipping away at school while working a steady job. The day of my 21st birthday arrived, November 15, 2002. All I wanted was to be around the people I loved and have a good time. That's exactly what I did. By the time the night was over, I ended staying the night with my boyfriend, Anthony. Do you see the pattern - how it seems Anthony popped up out of the blue? He's always there, in and out of my life.

At that time, we were back together; this time more serious than before. Anthony had gotten us a hotel room for the night of my birthday. That night we were talking, and the conversation turned to more serious topics - about life and the things we wished for, and things we needed to do to get to the next level in our lives. As the conversation progressed, we added God into the discussion, toying with if we thought He was really real or not. As we talked, and I rolled up a joint, something hit me like a force of lightening, down to my soul. I heard a voice say to me, "I'm going to show you why my people are the way they are." It was an awakening that seemed to make things so clear. Like an "aha" moment. Before this occurrence I had picked up the Bible so many times and could never get passed the first page. After that night, I began reading the Bible and saw what God was revealing about this life He'd given to us. My life instantly changed. The things I was used to doing no longer brought me pleasure. I had no desire for my past life, especially for smoking weed. TK and I were still dating, but he soon became a part of the old things I no longer had a desire for. All I wanted was to engulf myself into the Word. The more I sought the Word, the more I craved it. There was something specific that stood out to me. I didn't know it then, but eventually the knowledge of FORGIVENESS, which I was being shown, would be pertinent to my walk and the events to come.

I had always dreamed about things but never paid much attention to them until they came to pass. It blew my mind when I found myself in a place where I felt I had been before. It could've been an actual place, or maybe even a conversation. I would attribute it to déjà vu, which in the natural sense doesn't make sense, but when you're walking with the Lord you learn that dreams and visions are spiritual and prophetic. There was one dream that stayed with me. It was daytime, and I was around the corner from my home, standing on an island median in the middle of the street. My mom walked up to me, and I'm crying telling her, "He's gone." Since we only receive dreams in part, this dream made no sense to me. But the feeling of loss in that dream pierced my heart and made me feel sad. The feelings from that dream would soon resurface.

TK and I were still together - not as strong, but we were still together. Over the course of time, Anthony and I didn't always see eye to eye, and eventually our minds were elsewhere but we hadn't let each other go. Things started getting ugly between us, and one day I put myself in a bad situation where I could have been facing jail time for domestic violence. How did this happen? You see, when you don't let something go when you know you need to let it go, you put yourself in a situation that you may not be able to get out of. Even when it's painful, you have to let it go so that you don't hurt yourself even more in the process. I should have let TK go years before. I also learned that a soul tie will have you bound much longer than your heart and mind want to be, and it won't let you go.

Anthony and I had an argument about something that, to this day - fifteen years later, I can't remember because it was so trivial and all too familiar. I shouldn't have cared since it was my niece's first birthday. That, alone, was far more important. I was so hot-headed that after all the phone calls from him, I was angry and irritated and didn't care what happened. When in fact I should've seen the plot of the enemy, and known he was causing strife. I wanted to be done with this relationship after all the commotion, so we met up and the situation quickly escalated. One minute we were arguing, and the next I had slashed him in the face with a razor I had concealed in my hand. Within thirty minutes, I was being arrested on the front porch of my house. I figured I would get out immediately, but one phone call to my parents let me know that would not be the case. I would have to sit in jail for several days.

Tears welled up in my eyes and I told myself everything was going to be fine. I sat those days in that cell reading the Word, feeding my mind and my heart. For me, that was the best option since I was locked down for twenty-three hours of the day and only let out one hour for air. As I read, God showed me, by reiterating from his word, the importance of accepting responsibility for my actions. That way the consequences wouldn't seem so harsh. All those days as I sat in that jail cell waiting, I had made up in my mind that no matter the outcome after seeing the judge, I would be responsible for my actions - no matter what my intent was.

At release, it was time to move forward. One of the conditions of my release was the restraining order that was imposed against me. I was not to be within fifty feet of Anthony. But on April 22, 2004, I unintendedly violated the order. And that was the day my brother, Mych, was taken from my family, our friends, and me.

I say all that to say, we never know where life is going to take us, what it's going to show us, or what we will experience. We do know the Word says, "I can do all things through Christ who strengthens me." {NKJV Phil 4:13}

It also says, "I form the light and create darkness, I make peace and create calamity; I, the Lord, do all these things."

Am I completely healed from all of these traumatic events that have occurred in my life? No. I sometimes still question God as to why someone who I'd loved for so much of my life could so boldly murder my brother right in front of me. Yet, I still felt the need to forgive Anthony. Because of what Jesus, my Lord and Savior, did for me on the cross, it was clear why my heart was led to forgive Anthony. In no way am I saying what Anthony did was right. In all my wrongs, though, they may not look like Anthony's wrong doings, but to God they carry the same impact.

What God did for me through His son's death and resurrection, for all my transgressions, it warranted me to do the same for a person who hurt me in the most unimaginable way. It's clearly not understandable, but when you accept Christ as your savior and recognize what He did for you through His death, being on the giving end of forgiveness is the least you can do – at least it was for me. Every day I consider that the forgiveness we receive, and that's available to all of us, is so much bigger than we could ever imagine.

God's Word keeps me hopeful and trusting in Him that one day I will be with Him in paradise because His word says so. His word says I can do all things through Christ who strengthens me. It hurts and it's painful to have to forgive when a person has violated your trust, but we have a God who knows every offense.

> *"I said in my heart, God shall judge the righteous and the wicked, for there is a time for every purpose and for every work."*
>
> *ECC. 3:17 (NKJV)*

Building Your Fearless Faith Muscle:

1. Hold on to the word. Remember it, study it, trust it, and believe it. Had I not been in the word every day, thinking on the promises of God, I would have gone crazy and probably would have ended up in a mental asylum. But, holding steadfast to His word kept my mind in perfect peace.

2. Experiences are experiences. Don't let anyone tell you your experiences are small. What I went through was enough for me to trust God even when I didn't want to, and even when my flesh said it wasn't fair. Nothing has to be fair. Right is right, and wrong is wrong.

3. Trust His process. It's to build us up stronger than we've ever been, and it's all for our good.

4. Satisfy your soul in the Spirit of the Lord and see the awesomeness of God.

5. Learn how to fast and pray so that when the test and trials come, you can stand firm in your Fearless Faith.

CHAPTER 9

EVELYN ALEXANDER

Weathering the Storm Through Faith

"And we know that all things work together for good to them that love God, to them who are the called according to his purpose"

Romans 8:28

> *God works in "everything" – for our good. Remember, this does not mean that all that happens to us is good. Evil is prevalent in this world, but God can turn every circumstance around for our good. God is working to make us happy but more importantly to fulfill His purpose.*

At the age of forty-six, I was a happy wife, mother, employee, and learning Child of God. Life was good. My family and I were happy and content with where we were as a family and as individuals. We each had our own responsibilities and collective roles as we moved together toward our vision. Of course, there were the daily life experiences both good and bad, yet we were in our groove and making it.

Our daughter, Patrice, was doing well in her studies at a local community college and planning her move to a cosmetology course at the local big-name training facility. During this time in life she was in hot pursuit of the Lord and moved us all into action along with her on the path to living a life worth living.

It was during this time that Patrice shared not only with me, her dad, and her brother, Mych, that she was going to intentionally walk God's path for her life, she also shared and invited her boyfriend to come along. This news changed the direction for Patrice's life and ended a long-time relationship with her boyfriend. I was excited for her yet saddened by the break-up as he was the type of young man you would love to have as a son-in-law and given that I had known his family for many years was a plus. Even though their relationship had ended, Big Mych and he remained friends and hung out together on occasion. God has a way of positioning our lives and people in it to fulfill His purpose.

Big Mych – all six feet two inches, three hundred twenty pounds of him - possessed the heart of a teddy bear. He came into this world with a burst so powerful, my body was shaking so hard and fast I felt like a mountain about to erupt. When I first saw his face, he had this sweet but stern brow with soulful eyes.

It seemed like I turned around and he grew into his twentieth year of life. He had seen much, met many and had a love for the Lord only a few knew about from his words, but many knew about from his actions and presence.

On April 22, 2004 my husband, Ron, and I enjoyed our morning wake-up ritual. We shared our plans for the day, had our daily send-off kiss before I rushed out the door.

I arrived at my office. It seemed like the lunch hour came quickly that day. Since the sun was out and there was a nice breeze, I decided to eat outside. That hour, too, seemed to fly by, and it was time to get back to work.

Then came the call. "Honey, you better come home! Come quick! Big Mych's been shot." I dropped to my chair hearing the pain in my husband's voice. His pain ripped through my chest as the uncertainty in his voice made me question to myself if he was telling me the truth. He asked if I wanted him to come get me. I said, "No, I'll be there as quick as I can get there." I remember asking him if Mych was dead; he said in a hushed tone. "No, but…hurry."

My heart and my head went straight to my baby boy being dead. For a moment Fear crept into my spirit pushing Faith aside. I could barely stand to walk out of my office to face the inquiring eyes and questions from my staff. *"Evelyn! What's wrong? Do you need anything? Do we need to call someone? Can I drive you? Really, you shouldn't drive, let me drive you."* All I remember saying is, "No. I can make it. I know God will make sure of that."

The horrifying twenty-minute drive home was filled with numbness and prayer – yes, prayer. My faith muscle had been temporarily reactivated. "Thank you, Lord, for protecting my son. Thank you, Lord, for driving grace and speed. Thank you, Lord, for letting me find all is well…" as I felt the uncertainty, the fear of what I might find. With all the prayer I still felt the eerie feeling of something I could not, and did not, want to let set into my heart.

I rounded the corner by the park near our home noting that the sun was shining; there were people playing baseball and having fun in the park. I thought, Big Mych could not have been shot. There weren't any police cars, yellow tape, or emergency vehicles. As the words dragged across my brain, I saw the things I had hoped not to see. The police were actually there, and in the middle of the police was my beautiful daughter, her face full of tears and anguish. I jumped out the car and ran to her enveloping her like a mother hen would do her baby chick. We locked eyes sharing a look of deep pain, while in my mind I thought this could not be happening. Like any mother, I wanted to stay and see to her well-being and safety, but the first thing she mumbled was, "No, go mom! You need to get to the hospital…they just left with Mychael."

As I started toward my vehicle, my nephew, Lil "T," ran over and said, "No Aunty, you are not driving!" He took the keys from my hand while a friend of Patrice's escorted me to the passenger's seat. We headed around the corner to my house to see if Ron was there and ensure it was secure before heading to the county hospital. It was during this ride that I reflected on a conversation my son and I had the preceding day.

Big Mych had come to pick me up from work. He was so happy that he had qualified to join the cement mason's union. He had been working to clean up a couple of traffic tickets. Things were going well for him. I should say most things were going well. He also shared with me that he had attended a friend's funeral.

He said the church was so crowded that he had to sit on the front pew with the family. I said, "You must have been feeling some kind of way to sit in close proximity of the parents and watch them deal with the death of their child." I ended my statement saying, "That is why I always tell you to be safe. I just don't think I could live if something like that happened to you."

The next day Mychael called me at my office to ask if he could bring cash to me to purchase a counter check for him to send along with a bill he needed to pay. I told him, "Of course, I can do that, or I can pay the bill with my card and put the money in my bank." About twenty minutes later he brought the money down to my office along with the bill. I gave him back twenty dollars and told him not to be late picking his sister up from school and take the money to treat her to lunch. We giggled. I gave him a kiss and told him that I loved him. He responded with the same words, and he was off.

I shifted back to the moment as I heard my nephew asking, "Where should I park?" I saw the hospital emergency sign and instructed him to let me out there. I saw my husband moving toward me quickly as I approached the entrance. He was shaking his head no, and I started crying and mumbling, "No, no, no! Don't tell me he's gone! Don't tell me that!" I crumbled to my knees, my husband gently catching me before I hit the ground.

He gathered me and supported me as we walked back into the emergency area. The whole section was overflowing with Big Mych's friends. Everyone was crying and looking at us as if they were asking; "What shall we do? How are we going to handle this? Tell us he's okay. Help us!"

We shared hugs and words of encouragement while at the same time being escorted to a private room where a doctor, one of Big Mych's life friends, clergy, and now us sat waiting. It seemed like hours had ticked by but when I looked at the clock we had only been there for ten minutes. I prayed silently and aloud for God's continued mercy on my beloved son's life. *"God, help me, show me who you are in this instance, strengthen me, I need you. I know you, God, are in control. God, your will be done. Thank you, God, for what you are doing through this situation. Thank you, God, for covering us all."* I looked around the room at my husband and Mych's friends and prayed, "Keep us God! Keep me, God!" There seemed to be stillness in the air and a decreasing of the troubled spirits in the room.

As the doctor entered the room I quickly looked toward my husband to ensure he was near. I saw anticipation in his eyes as he moved closer to me. Then I looked at the doctor before he started to speak and could feel nothing but bad news coming as he said the words no one wants to here, "I'm sorry… we have done all we could do…."

My knees weakened, and my body went limp. I hit the floor pleading, **"God help me to accept your will!"** I was sobbing so deeply, through so much hurt, that I couldn't catch my breath. My heart was in so much pain I couldn't stand it and I was hoping the tears were washing away the unwanted anguish.

Those tears were the beginning of the cleansing of my body, my mind, and my soul so I could continue to live through the fear of never seeing my son's beautiful face again. I cried so hard. Ron did like any other loving husband and went into protective mode. He had dropped to my side and wrapped his arms around me. I began to shake him off; not because I didn't need him, but it felt as if he was smothering me, separating me from something. As he removed his arms, I felt a tender peacefulness cover my shoulders and move down my back, to my feet. A cloak of peace and tenderness covered me, and to this day I still feel that covering. **The Peace of GOD was the blanket- -the DRIVING PURPOSE behind my thoughts and actions. It was an encounter with His Presence.** It was the precise moment when faith replaced fear, and I knew God would carry me through the darkest season of my life.

From the moment I felt covered, I knew that something unique would happen out of this senseless pain, this loss. But what? I rode home silently from the hospital in shock, numbness, and disbelief. I found little words to say, and as we arrived home from the hospital I knew the word of Big Mych's passing had spread like wildfire. There was a sea of family, neighbors, friends and people wanting to know who, what, and why.

They were angry and hurt by his death. I, honestly, wanted to lead the pack to get this person who took my son. He was my daughter's long-time boyfriend and a family friend. He had taken one of our precious gems. I knew it was not time for me to share my raw feelings - I didn't want a battle or another life taken. If this was about me I would have shared what I was feeling and thinking, things like… go get him and do as you will or bring him to me so I could ask, *what were you thinking? What was going through your mind to go to our neighborhood park, where a high school baseball game was in progress, where you and all of us have spent fun times making memories, and where kids were playing. Why would you meet up with Patrice and Mych and start waving a gun at them? Then you chase Mych around a tree until he slips, stand over him, and shoot him in the back while he is lying face down? What were you thinking?* I would remind him how I have backed him, how I have treated him with kindness and welcomed him into our home, our family. I would have reminded him that we were family and ask how he could harm a family member, especially Mych. I would have yelled, screamed, cried and put the pain of loss on him through words and tears so he could experience first-hand how angry and hurt I was. I might have even punched him in his chest or twisted his ears; but I definitely would have made sure he was immediately taken into custody. I can honestly say that I never wanted him physically harmed or wanted to take his life. Those thoughts never entered into my mind or spirit. As I moved out of those thoughts, what came to mind is that violence never solved anything or brought anyone back from the dead; but prayer and faith does help put life into perspective.

God, help me to say the words to bring peace and understanding, is what I silently prayed. I opened my mouth and out came the words that were not my first thoughts. "Thank you everyone for your love and support. I know you are all mad and even angry, but violence is not what I want to come from this. We just lost our son, and we don't want to lose another person. Please, don't any of you get yourself in trouble by going after this young man. Believe me, he is scared not only of you but what he has done. I need you all to take care of one another and to make sure the loss of Big Mych's life not be taken in vain through giving up your life. Pray for us, yourself, and this young man. I forgive him and I need each of you to find it in yourself to do the same."

I heard lots of under-the-breath mumbling. One person spoke out, "We know what you mean, and we will do our best." As the days went on, some did as we asked, and others to this day are stuck in the fallout from Mych's death.

When the crowd of witnesses -- (like Job's wife and friends) wanted us to be angry and take vengeance into our own hands-- we showed the purpose of God and forgave. "Do not take vengeance into your own hands but vengeance is Mine, I will repay or forgive those who hurt and despitefully use you or your Heavenly Father will not forgive you." (Romans 12:19)

For the next two weeks, it was family arriving, friends dropping by.... people, people, people everywhere. Though we had people who loved us around for support when I really needed that soul touching help, I knew where to go get it and I would sneak off to my room to cry and pray; then reemerge with that peaceful covering. No one understood how I could be at peace and exhibit it to help others at a time like that. All I can say is the more I was a blessing, and blessed God through the situation, the more God blessed me in the situation.

Even though I was in shock, in agony like no other, not able to truly feel anything - there was this forever presence of being in a protected bubble. No matter how hard the sadness, anger, hurt, and pain pushed to set in; those emotions never got to my soul or spirit. I felt and knew that no matter what actions we took moving forward, my emotions needed to be purposeful; not only to meet our family's needs but to share in the spreading of the goodness through this tragedy. During the many encounters of grief-stricken family and friends, it became evident that our attitude and actions were one of the strongest catalysts that helped to keep our neighborhood and extended community as a sanctuary for people to process their grief. Grieving through faith and the word of God allowed us to be in His ordained place in a tragic situation. I knew He would continue to take care of us.

∾⎯⎯∾

Forgiveness is the key. It truly is for you, not those who have done harm. I should have been stone cold out of my mind because of the love and life that was brutally stripped from me. I could have walked around bitter, talking ugly, or pursuing revenge. However, I knew none of that would bring Big Mych back. Would being angry make me happier and more at peace? What would Big Mych want me to do? What does the Bible say? What's the result I wanted? I could not come up with a result that encouraged me to pursue anger and revenge. No, that would not fill the void left behind. Kicking and fighting, I accepted the fact that pay-back was and is not mine to give.

> *"Dearly beloved, avenge not yourselves, but rather give place unto wrath:*
> *for it is written, Vengeance is mine; I will repay, saith the Lord.*
> *(Romans 12:19 - KJV)*

I toyed around with ideas of dispensing the same pain I was feeling through some evil action. I thought about telling his mom what a dog her son was (along with a few other choice words). I thought about telling her how she would suffer from the recklessness of her son. I wanted her to recognize her loss and mine too! Not finding that peace that surpasses all understanding in doing any of those things, I encouraged myself to continue to trust in God and have faith that God had a plan.

> *"Trust in the Lord with all thine heart; and lean not unto thine own*
> *understanding*
> *(Proverbs 3:5, KJV)*

Forgiveness is not easy. It took every ounce of my being and passion for my son to openly and freely call out to God to help me. I was looking for help in every area of the situation, and I knew in the deepest part of my heart that there was not a human being, kind word or action that could give me what I needed to pull through this and still live, love, and laugh. So, I did what I was learning... cast my pain, hurt, distrust, anger... and every piece of baggage that I had on God through prayer, thought, and action. No, I didn't go into some long wordy prayer; it was just a simple heartfelt cry.

I am so in awe of how letting go and letting God be in control of your heart, mind, mouth and by truly leaning on Him will take what was meant to harm you and turn it around to have profound impact for God's glory.

I feared what life would be like without Big Mych. I could no longer see his face, his smile, or feel his good-hearted presence. To this day, I still feel as if a portion of me has been torn away; I just don't feel whole in my heart. I think about all that is no longer whole such as his daughter, who had just turned one; he didn't have the opportunity to raise her, get married, or continue his relationships with his family, friends, and community. I am sure that Mych had a relationship with God and is resting in Heaven. Knowing that Big Mych is with God and we will reunite is a phenomenal thought.

One of the defining moments of what forgiveness will do for you and others became evident through the legal process. The trial was four days long; and even though we attended as a unified family, it was Patrice who had an active role as a witness for the defense and I submitted the "impact statement." The impact statement gives the weight of the tragedy on our lives, our community, friends, and neighbors. Of course, I never thought I would have the need to write an impact statement - no one ever does. When it came time to write it, we all struggled. Each of us was at our own level of grief and forgiveness, so to write an impact statement that was inclusive of all our feelings took deep thought and consideration. We were conflicted by what punishment was deserved. However, one agreement remained; we did not want a harsh punishment. We believed that the shooting was a momentary lapse in judgment and that he would suffer the rest of his days because of it. We had to remember that we weren't the only family impacted in this.

Impact Statement Excerpt:

We feel great concern and worry over what will happen to Anthony should he be incarcerated into a system that is meant to rehabilitate, but is very well known for doing the opposite. Anthony had the bad misfortune of losing control of himself which resulted in the worse outcome one could possibly be a part of – taking the life of someone you love.

I have cried many a night since this happened not only for my son, but also for Anthony.

I can only imagine what has been going through his mind and his heart. If not for this misfortune I believe that he would be doing something constructive with his life.

I am having a very hard time knowing that my family will be a part of the reason that someone we consider to be family may be imprisoned for a period of time.

We feel that Anthony could be better served by being placed in a program or institution that would allow him to deal with the guilt he is feeling and the lack of control that got him where he is today. He should speak to others to encourage them to stay in control, not take actions that will result in such devastation, about the misery he feels after having done such a thoughtless act and the impact one's actions has on family, friends and the community.

In our opinion, no amount of prison time will bring my son back. It won't make those that are suffering feel any better. It won't replace the love my son had for his daughter, his family, friends or community. Most importantly it won't do honor to our son who we know would not want to have Anthony experience such a bleak future.

Sad to say, Anthony will be emotionally and mentally imprisoned by his actions for the rest of his life. Physical imprisonment will only serve to compound his misery.

For these realistic reasons, my tears and concerns run deep for Anthony. We truly forgive him and are concerned about his well-being. We hate that there will be another life lost because of this very unfortunate incident. I still want to hug him and tell him things will be okay no matter what the final outcome.

With deepest respect

Sincerely,

Ron, Evelyn and Patrice

Going through the legal process did not help to improve my husband's heart, mind, or soul. His anger was a lot slower to subside. He still has a light undercurrent that flows through his mind, which impacts his desire for life and trusting others. He works daily to remove those demons. After thirteen years, it was in April 2017 that he visited Big Mych's resting place for the first time since his burial. I praise God for His diligence and patience.

Patrice apologized for years for bringing the young man into our lives. She carried a burden of guilt, and I still think she harbors some defeating burden of responsibility. She still struggles with entrusting her heart to a young man; yet she continues to put her faith in God to provide her needs.

For me, from day one I had forgiven our family friend; so, the trial represented the world's requirement and desire for justice. Justice without mercy is injustice. To show mercy is not to put the person under condemnation. At the heart of justice is mercy.

> *For he shall have judgment without mercy, that hath shewed no mercy; and mercy rejoiceth against judgment.*
>
> *(James 2:13 -KJV)*

I believe that the judge felt our pain and understood our dilemma as the young man was charged with second degree murder, found guilty and sentenced to seventeen years, with three years of probation upon release, the medium level of punishment for that crime.

Everyone who witnessed us go through our situation while still acknowledging God as our strength can now choose to do the same. Forgiveness involves attitude and action. If you find it difficult to *feel* forgiving toward someone who hurt you, try responding with kind actions and/or words. Many times, you will find that right actions lead to right feelings.

> *Like Job-- we did not curse or question God-- we just worshipped Him. "In all of this, Job sinned not, nor charged God foolishly.*
>
> *(Job 1:22, KJV)*

Our attitude was— *"I will bless the Lord at all times: his praise shall continually be in my mouth.* (Psalm 34:1, KJV)

We live the new normal now. We have many loving memories of Big Mych. Our beautiful fifteen-year old granddaughter is the embodiment of her father in physique and demeanor.

I just can't help praising God for His greatness in our situation. I bet my church family got a little tired of me praising God and sharing the testimony of what He did during that time. Certain songs like "No Weapon" or "Hold Out (Sun is Gonna Shine)" would send me into a frenzy of praise and tears without shame. I took every opportunity that came my way (and there were plenty) to share my love for God and how He brought us through. I took it as an opportunity to fulfill God's purpose of peace.

God can't bless you when you put yourself in a position where He can't bless you. As we look to God to continue to make sense of our loss, I have not had, and I believe I will not have the desire to ask God why it happened. Being a believer does not mean that you don't go through the pains associated with death. God is proactive about our struggles and storms. God will hear your groaning, your deep moan that indicates you are in pain, whether it's the sounds of crying, the feeling of despair, feelings you can't put to words. God helps us through our weakness. *"Likewise the Spirit also helpeth our infirmities: for we know not what we should pray for as we ought; but the Spirit itself maketh intercession for us with groanings which cannot be uttered."* (Romans 8:26 – KJV)

God values your groaning, your pain. What groaning can you make available to God through the Holy Spirit to allow Him to be involved in your situation?

Christ reminds us that through faith and belief we can rise above anything. We can move from fear to faith, and then to Fearless Faith. No matter what you are going through, God has a plan for your life and purposely moves to implement His plan. He did it for me, so why wouldn't He do it for you?

"For I know the thoughts that I think toward you, saith the Lord,
thoughts of peace, and not of evil, to give you an expected end."
(Jeremiah 29:11, KJV)

Building Your Fearless Faith Muscle:

When you don't know what to do – can't figure it out, go back to basics!

By now we all know there is not a step-by-step manual on how to "make it" through life after a tragedy. All of us feel, react, and respond differently - that's human nature.

What I did find is absolute direction, support, love, grace, and mercy in putting it all in God's capable hands. I *"Recklessly Leaned on the Lord."* There is nothing that I was not feeling, thinking, hearing, and needing that I did not open to God. My heart and ears were and are open.

1. God's scriptures are many. His will is the only one that will get you where He wants you to be. In those moments when you are missing the one you cherished, read God's word! Specifically, ones pertaining to your need(s). If it's fear, read about fear. If it's love, read about love. If it's faith, read about faith, etc. While, and after reading, focus on what God's word has put in your mind and on your heart. *"Rest, Trust, and Believe."* I made time to rest in the comfort, to determine in my mind and heart to trust and believe in the scriptures, God's words, to help me make it through.

2. Prayer is the language of and to God. As I lean, rest, trust, and believe I take action to speak to God in His language; simple and with gratitude. Thanking God even though I had not fully understood how He was working throughout my loss and grief. He provided a continuing feeling of peace in my spirit. It has allowed me to not become the bitter and grief-stricken person I had prayed not to become. I feel *"Fearless, Faithful, and Free,"* and that is a way of life for me today and always. I have no fear because I know that I am in control of my faith and God is in control of my fate. This helps me be free in living life through love and purpose.

3. Storms are worse when they come without warning. We go to church; we do good in hope of being exempt from storms. There are no guarantees against these unexpected storms. Joseph went to prison; Job lost everything; and Daniel was in the lion's den. Just know that God is always in the storm with you (us). Faith is God's prescription for grief. It's the means by which we make it through. Faith calms grief; dispels despair. Allow yourself to recover through the awesome power of God. Allow God to be sovereign in this, and all, situations.

CHAPTER 10

ALEXUS DOVER

Blessings in the Cursed

"You shall not bow down to idols or worship them, for I, the Lord your God am a jealous God, punishing the children for the sins of the fathers to the third and fourth generation of those who hate me."

Exodus 20:5

Growing up I heard about family generational curses. My mom spoke of it often and her desire to see the chains broken. Generational curses - those negative patterns of behavior thought to be passed on from ancestors - holds a family in spiritual bondage. I thought that I would be the one to break the cycle. As fate would have it, I became its victim - the same victim that my mother had also been at my age. At the age of twelve, I, like my mom, was sexually assaulted by a family member. The violation continued until I was seventeen.

Confused and not sure what to do, I held onto the secret. In silently carrying the shame, I was continuing the cycle of abuse that would forever change my perception about my abuser, my relationship with my family, and ultimately shape my relationship with God. I knew God loved me, but I was confused because I did not understand how a God so loving would permit this to happen. Having grown up in a family full of praying women, I've always had a connection to God, but not on a deep, personal level. I didn't truly know how to activate my faith. But I did know that God's love was greater than anything I had experienced at my age and things would have to change.

Not long after celebrating nineteen years on the Earth, I made the bold decision to join the U.S. Navy. I was young and ready to start a new chapter of my life. One of the pages in that new chapter became my son's father. Like most damaged girls, I wanted to be loved. I thought I found that when I met him. He was so caring, sweet, extremely charming, and always encouraging me to be better than the day before. Continuously giving me affirmations, and always willing to give me the attention I needed. He was nothing like what I was used to. He was very honest and forthcoming. So, I thought. There were no red flags and no reason for alarm – at the time. In the beginning, he wasn't argumentative, and even when we did argue he was always the one who calmed the situation (and me) down. I thought he was someone I could confide in, a lover and a friend.

After a year of dating, we decided to say, "I do!" on December 13, 2013. Yes, we were young. We were in love. We gave no thought to what it really meant to be married and become one flesh, as it is written in Mark 10:8. Everything felt so right. I thought that he was my better half – my soul mate. I didn't think about asking God if this was the husband for me. I felt like he was my husband. I felt like I could discern if that was what I needed or didn't need; and if I felt like this was the man then nothing else mattered. I was in love.

In an alcohol-induced text message, I told my parents that I married a man they had never met. You might be thinking, "Where are your morals? Where are the values your parents instilled?" Well, to me, my parents had instilled the value of meeting someone and having them ask for my hand in marriage. I didn't see a need for their pre-approval or consideration of him. I knew what I wanted. As an adult, I didn't need anyone's permission to get married. They were surprisingly supportive and told me they would support whatever I felt was best for me. That support gave me more confidence, made me comfortable in my decision, and gave me some assurance that I was on the right path toward marital bliss.

Shortly after we got married, my husband was discharged from the military due to alcohol abuse and underage drinking. In a very brief period, I had to find and furnish an apartment; and get my husband a ticket to San Diego where I was stationed. Everything was in place and I believed that since we would be living together, we could be a "real" married couple. Without knowing his flaws or his shortcomings (nor he of mine), I had hoped living together would be a breeze. We had been stationed apart for so long, I truly believed that absence would make our hearts grow fonder. I was sadly mistaken.

I found out that my ex-husband was cheating on me. The relationship with the other woman began just after we were married. I also discovered that he might have fathered a child with her. Heartbroken couldn't describe what I experienced. I was betrayed. How could this happen? We had only been married four months. I knew that this wasn't the ideal marriage, but if I gave up so soon could I really say I had given it my all? I was determined I wasn't going to allow the enemy to take my marriage. I decided to stick it out and work on my marriage; and with that came some ultimatums.

"Dylan," I called his name one Sunday after returning from church. "You get some help and start going to church, or I'm filing for divorce."

He decided to get some help and we were worshipping together. This new thing only lasted a short while. I had to participate in a Naval training exercise in Hawaii. I sailed out in July. August rolled in with the devastating news that my grandmother had lost her battle with ovarian cancer. She was my rock. Thousands of miles away from home and my mom, I was shattered! It seemed life had been snuffed out of me. I didn't know how to deal with the loss while dealing with a breaking marriage.

There is an old wives' tale that says when one life is taken a new life is born. It proved to be true for me. Hours after I find out about my grandmother's death, I found out I was five weeks pregnant. I was so excited that the first person I called was my husband then my mother. Her reaction was rather bland, dry and discouraging. It made me think it was the wrong time to have a baby.

Was this pregnancy announcement – and the pregnancy – too much to handle with the passing of my grandmother? Our family, as we knew it, would never be the same. Grandmother was the glue that held our family together. She took pride in being the matriarch of our family and setting the example of Jesus Christ. I can only wish that someday I would have the same impact on others.

Once the military confirmed my pregnancy, I was flown back home to San Diego to work shore duty until the birth of my son. My return home was met with immediate challenges. We were soon to be homeless due to nonpayment of rent. I was floored! I'd been sending my husband money for the bills. Apparently, he was using the money for his recreational purposes like drugs and going out partying with his friends. He didn't even communicate that we were going to be homeless. I was raised to be self-sufficient, to depend on no one but the Lord. I took pride in being twenty-one with my own place, own car, and doing well in a promising career. Within a millisecond it would all be snatched from me. How could he be so careless? Thoughtless? The alcohol was one of the many demons that began to show. Here I was newly pregnant, grieving, facing eviction and all my husband could think about was what was best for him and his habit. All I could think was how could I possibly go to God with this? I didn't go to Him before I got married. So why go now?

By now, you might be thinking I should have let this marriage go and moved on. For me, divorce was not an option. This was another "stand by your man" moment. Besides, I asked myself what type of person I would be to give up versus working through the problems. I did not see the problems as clear flashing red lights or yellow warning tape. It did not occur to me that God was trying to show me that this wasn't the man he called to be my husband or the father of my child.

Determined to make the best out of a disastrous situation, I found a solution. I moved us into a new apartment, and we were seemingly on a fresh start. Dylan found work driving trucks at night, while I worked the same shift on base. What seemed to be a perfect solution became the biggest reality check and worse nightmare. A friend of his was released from the military and unbeknownst to me Dylan agreed that he could stay with us. Three adults in a two-bedroom apartment; one room for the nursery, and the other for us. The deal was he could stay for thirty days and then he would be on his way to Florida.

I knew nothing about Dylan's friend, but, shockingly, I trusted my husband's judgment. Three days. That's how long he had been living there before Dylan quit his job and began to drink and heavily use drugs. It would only be a few more days before Dylan was gone more than he was home. I started praying and asking God to cover our marriage, finances and our home. To give me the strength I needed to push through since now I would be the sole provider.

Things started to spiral out of control. Arguments became more frequent. We were becoming more and more distant. I was under so much stress I couldn't focus at work. Everything that I thought I had control of was slowly starting to fall apart. In one heated argument, he shook me and hit me because he said I wasn't listening. The first thing I thought was, "*God, please don't let him hurt my baby.*"

With tears and fear in my eyes, I pleaded, "Dylan, please stop! You're going to hurt the baby." His response, "The baby can't even feel this yet. You'll be fine."

Shocked doesn't begin to describe what I felt. I had never seen that side of Dylan. Perhaps I was so blinded by what I thought was love, I didn't want to see that side of him. I kept telling myself things would get better. I thought with counseling and prayer things would change, but it seemed to worsen. I knew I couldn't go to my mom with this. What would she think of me? Would she help or judge me? Here's where my faith should've activated; instead it dwindled. It felt like the more I prayed for peace in our marriage, the less God answered. I began to believe God had given up on me and I was stuck to fix the mess I created. The arguments intensified and became physical more often than not. I was literally a prisoner in my own home and didn't even realize it. One of our arguments – in the car - got so bad he hopped out of the car into the middle of traffic. He was banging on the car, threatening to break the windows. We were still on base and people were staring. Embarrassed, I broke down and cried. I pleaded for him to stop – he persisted.

I pulled over to the side of the road, with him running after my car; and even punching my passenger side mirror. He was angry that I took his phone. All I could do was cry and wonder how I got to this point. I was scared to go home. I was scared of my husband. Base officers arrived and handcuffed him. He resisted and even fought them. He threatened to get me when he came home. One of the officers asked if I felt I would be safe. I knew he was angry; and I knew he meant what he said. Still, I responded, "Yeah."

The guard, I guess seeing something in my face, said, "I'm going to issue a ban on his name, so he can't come onto any military installation until you give birth to your son."

You would think I would be thankful; instead I was embarrassed and broken. Dylan got out, apologized and said he had acted like a fool. I believed him and things got worse. I started working days, and I would come home to find his "new" friends in my house. The refrigerator was always empty. I was constantly pawning things to make sure there was money for gas for my car and food in the house only to come home to nothing. I started stealing food from the convenience store. Finally, I realized the weight of the situation when I had to pawn something that mattered so much to me - my mom's ring.

It hurt me every day to look in the mirror and know that I was living in hell. I was constantly fighting, broke and crying. I was in a corner and didn't know how to get out or who to talk to. I didn't know if I should call my family. I feared I might be judged because of the way I started my family. I sought help from the chaplain. He assured me that God hadn't forgotten about me, and that He saw what I was going through. His advice - have faith and trust that the situation at hand was only temporary. Although I was listening, I couldn't help but think God didn't want to hear me. In my state of deactivated faith, I had veered so far away from Him and done so many things. Surely, I thought God was not interested in hearing about all of my bad decisions. God could not be interested in hearing me tell Him how much I needed Him to get me out of my mess.

Are you beginning to question, "How could you be in this book that's speaking on having fearless faith and here you are fearful, doubtful and faithless?" The thing is - I'm human. I had moments where I believed what the enemy planted in my mind. I felt since I couldn't see the promises God had for me, why should I continue to believe they were truly there. I lost sight of true faith and in turn I fell into the enemy's way of thinking. Funny how God has a way of showing up when you least expect Him.

Stressed beyond measure and hardly eating, I went into labor at thirty-six weeks. I pleaded with God to let the baby be healthy. Dylan, still in his own world, was oblivious to what was happening. A friend drove me to the hospital. My water broke in the middle of the floor as we walked in and I was admitted immediately. Dylan showed up (with another of his new friends), both smelling like weed. The nurse gave him two options: leave and change his clothes or leave and don't come back. He came back about four in the morning. I gave birth to my healthy son, Preston; who is the light of my life.

When I looked at him and held him in my arms, I knew God heard my cries. I felt such peace, calmness and unconditional love. That moment was short lived. What should have been a time of healing and bonding with my son, became one of interrogation and fighting. Child Protective Services had been notified of a potential problem, and they came in to determine if our home was safe for the well-being of my child. They drilled me about Dylan's drug use, the use of drugs by others in the house, and all sorts of hazards.

When the interrogation was done, I fell onto the bed crying. "God! How could this happen? How could I allow myself to get so deep into this hole? What am I going to go home to?"

We didn't have a bed, car seat, or stroller for the baby. We didn't have many clothes, no bathing items - nothing! I sank into a pit of depression; and I didn't know how to come out of it. By God's mercy, my neighbor heard that I went into early labor and gave us an extra car seat she was holding on to. I cried, relieved, I couldn't leave the hospital without a car seat and I had no money. Preston and I were going home. Now, you would think, or at least I thought, that the arrival of the baby would help him change. That daddy would make new, positive friends. Yet, the devil stayed busy and reminded me that he would not stop just because I wanted him too.

Still in the same vicious cycle; but now seeing the presence of the generational curse of mental, emotional and physical abuse fully displayed in my life, I had to make another decision. I had a choice to either stay in that miserable place or get out. I didn't see a way out; so, I asked him to move. I had no money. I still hadn't told my parents anything about the hellish situation. When I spoke with them, I always convinced them that we were in a "great place." Our first night home Dylan agreed to keep the baby while I got some rest. That gave me hope. I was sadly mistaken. The baby's cries woke me up. It seemed he had been crying for a long time. Finally, I woke up and there was Dylan passed out on the floor. I took the baby out of his rocker and kicked Dylan as hard as I could. He had ingested so much narcotics that he was in a stupor.

I comforted my son, rocking him back to sleep. Then I drug my drugged-up husband into the bathroom to run water over him, and make sure he was breathing. This nightmare was not going to end. I felt like my prayers had fallen on deaf ears. The next day Dylan's mom arrived. What I thought would be a lifeline turned out to be a silent bystander. She had not once questioned us on the damages in our apartment or how they had come about. I was beginning to think this wasn't a shock to her. The vibe she gave was an "out of sight out of mind" kind of thing and that bothered me. Shortly after that, my mom arrived. We were all supposed to go to dinner. Dylan, in typical fashion, said he had to make a run with his friend and said he would be back in an hour. An hour turned into three hours. I was fed up and I told him we weren't waiting on him.

I went out to get dinner for us and when I got back my mom said Dylan came running into the house like a mad man, asked where I was and seemed surprised that we hadn't gone out as originally planned. This caused another argument which got way out of control and he ended up leaving. Before he left, he walked his mom to her rental car. It was her last night in town, and I'm sure he wanted to say a private goodbye and convince her that things would be alright. While that took place outside, inside I continued to act as if nothing ever happened, as if his drug-induced temper tantrum didn't just happen in front of not only his mom, but mine and my seven-year old niece. Crazy as this may sound; I still wanted to put up a united front. The united front – that night – wasn't necessary because Dylan said goodbye to his mom and disappeared.

I went looking for him in the middle the night. I found him high and drunk yet again. When we returned home my mom called me to the living room and asked me if Dylan was on drugs. Not wanting her to think negative of him, I told her no. My mom knows me better than anybody in this world, so she knew I was lying, but she let it go. The next day while showering, Dylan decided he would apologize and talk to me about what happened the night before, like he'd done repeatedly. During the conversation, I heard my mom call my name. "*Alexus!*" She yelled repeatedly. Dylan and I were in the back conversing about the night before. Mom's voice rang loudly again and this time it moved me to action. I hurried past Dylan into the living room where my mom stood. She was furious because two of Dylan's "friends" had come over and one of them knocked on the door but before my mom could answer, he had turned the knob and entered as if it was his place. My mom had a look on her face that I knew all too well. I couldn't speak.

"Who is this fool? He just walked in here like he lives here," she screamed. Then another of Dylan's friends jumped over the patio. I looked out back, and sure enough, there were his homeboys, Jared and Vince, outside smoking cigarettes. Jared waltzed back into the house and began speaking to my mom very casually. I was bothered and slightly confused. *What just happened?* As usual, when I brought it to Dylan's attention, he played it off like it was nothing and went out back to hang with his friends. I got dressed and decided to take my mom and niece out to see San Diego. On the way to the car, my mom shared with me that she and my niece didn't feel safe staying in my home.

126 • FEARLESS FAITH

She said that she wanted to go to a hotel. I was heartbroken to say the least.

"Mom, why?" I asked.

"Because," she told me, "I am not used to people just walking into someone else's home without being welcomed in. These guys are too comfortable and act as if they live here. Is this how you run your household? Are his friends free to come and go as they please?" Mom had a look of sadness mixed with fear on her face.

"I'll talk to Dylan again mom," I said.

At this point, I knew something had to give. Either I was going to sacrifice my ties with my family or end my marriage. After a long heart to heart talk, mom agreed to stay. We went out to eat and I took them to the border of Mexico. We had a good time shopping and enjoying our time together. On the way home, my mom looked and me and told me how much she loved me.

Then she asked the question that I knew was soon to come. "Is Dylan abusive to you?"

"No, I said quickly." I knew right then, mom saw right through me. She always knows when I am being untruthful.

"Lex," she said softly, "I know the signs. I've lived through it. I'll do anything in this world for my children. I'll even go to the ends of the Earth to save you. But, you have to first be willing to accept the fact that your husband is a drug addict and an abuser. It's not going to get any better. You have a son to think about. You don't have to stay and take this. I raised you better than this."

Deep down inside I wanted to say, "Mommy, I want to leave." On the outside, what I said was, "It's ok Mommy. I'll be fine."

"OK," mom said. "But before I leave tomorrow I want to sit down with you and Dylan."

The next morning, mom summoned Dylan and I to the living room. What I thought would be a conversation for understanding and growth turned into a heated discussion between Dylan and my mom. I watched them go back and forth. Dylan had taken Preston out of his seat and was shaking him furiously.

His anger was getting the best of him and he was shaking and patting my baby just a little too hard. It scared me. I had an epiphany that one day shaking and patting would become hitting and throwing. I didn't want that for my son. He yelled at my mom, but mom didn't back down. Little did he know my mom was no pushover and his yelling didn't move her. She was firm when she spoke, and she told Dylan in no uncertainty what would happen if something happened to me or Preston. Dylan placed Preston back in his seat and stormed out of the house. After what seemed like an eternity, it was time for my mom to get ready to head to the airport. The drive seemed longer than before. The silence spoke volumes and I knew mom was upset. When we got to the airport, mom reassured me again when I was ready to leave, she would be there. I kissed her goodbye and headed back home with my son.

Dylan was sitting on the couch when I opened the door. I had barely removed my shoes when he went in on me. "You let your mom come into our home and disrespect me," he yelled. "You didn't try to defend me at all." He kept yelling, and there was something in his eyes that didn't feel right. He had the look of a rabid dog. He started throwing the baby's toys around and kicked my son's bedroom door in. I believed that night I was going to die. He was so enraged. Punching the wall and destroying whatever he could. Once he left the house I locked the bedroom door; I broke down and cried. I was completely broken, and it was starting to show.

After I put my son to sleep I went into the other room, and I fell to my knees and cried out to my Father. When I say I cried, I mean - I cried. This wasn't a silent sob; this was a loud painful cry. "God, I know you said you'd never leave me nor forsake me. God, I need you. I've tried it without you and I can't do this by myself. God, I'm so tired of this pain I feel. I'm tired of feeling alone; I don't want to be empty. I'm tired of feeling like I'm less than who you've called me to be. God, I just want you to come into my life and take over. Lord I know that you can do exceedingly and God I'm asking you to forgive me for accepting abuse as love, for replacing you with pride. God heal me. Touch my heart; don't let it harden." Once I started to release all that anger and the pain I felt; I promise you it was like God was in the room with me. I felt something nudging me to my Bible. Randomly, I opened it, and there was the answer to my prayers. Acts 16:31: "They replied, Believe in the Lord Jesus and you will be saved-you and your household." I knew that I wanted more for my son and I couldn't live that way anymore.

The next day Dylan went out as usual. I stayed at home with the baby. Out of nowhere, I heard a pounding at my door. It was the police. They asked if I was okay and if my husband was home. I assured them that I was fine and that he had just left to run some "errands." One of the officers explained that my mom had called all the way from Texas and begged them to make sure that I was okay because I had not responded to her calls. I reassured them that my son and I were fine, and I would give her a call. Once they left I couldn't help but cry. At his point, I knew God not only heard me, but He sent the lifeline I'd been praying for - my mom.

"Be strong," I heard Jesus whisper to my anxious heart. "I am with you," Jesus said. "Do not be afraid. Do not allow your circumstances to derail the plans I have for your life. Press in and press on. At this moment, I felt like I was on the verge of a faith crisis. Like at any moment my faith would fail me and I would be overtaken. I was afraid, but I knew at that moment I had to leave my marriage. My mom was in fear for my life over two thousand miles away, and here I was living in it and couldn't see the damage that it was doing. Damage not only to me, but also to my son. I called my job and let them know that I was going to be leaving for Texas for a few weeks and that I was in an abusive relationship for the past two years. To my surprise, they were helpful, comforting and told me to do whatever it took to get on the right path. They even offered to help me. I fell to my knees thanking God for helping me to move past the fear and embarrassment. He had a plan to save His child.

I called my parents and my dad told me to pack my things because they had purchased a plane ticket. I had no plan, I was just winging it, but I knew it had to be done. I began to question myself. *Am I doing the right thing? What if I have this all wrong? He just needs help. I can help him.* I teetered on the edge of staying there with my abusive husband and running as fast as I could to get to my mommy. I felt helpless. *God, help me!* I was afraid. Fear or freedom is what I pondered in my head. Now I know scripture but at this moment I needed to be specific. I needed God to speak to me in a way that I knew it was Him. I called my mom and she answered on the first ring. "Mom, I'm scared," I cried. "I don't want Dylan to figure out my plans to leave but a part of me wants to stay and help him."

"You have to help yourself first. You have a baby to think about," my mom lovingly scolded. "Go and read Psalm 27. The Lord is your light and your salvation. You don't have to fear Dylan or anyone else. Fear is not of God. It's only when we act out of fear that we make wrong choices. Fear is a spirit of the enemy, but freedom is offered to us by Jesus."

At that moment, I knew I had to choose fear or freedom. I chose freedom. I chose Fearless Faith in Jesus that would bring me my freedom. The next day my good friend, Jackson, came over to help me pack my things and store my car while I was in Texas. I confided in her about the fights and the constant abuse, and that leaving was my only way out. I told her that I let pride get in the way of asking for help. I felt like if I kept asking for help, I would be a burden to others and I didn't want that. In true Jackson fashion, she showed me empathy and opted to kick Dylan's behind at the same time. As much as I would have loved that, I knew God had bigger plans for him. With everything packed, and a destination in sight, I came up with a lie to get out of the house without looking suspicious. I made my getaway.

Once I made it to Texas, I received a call from Dylan asking when I would be home. I told him that we flew to Texas to visit my mom and we wouldn't be home for a while. He started crying and screaming that I took our son, I ruined his life, I broke our family. For a minute, I started to believe that he was right. That I broke up our family, ruined my son's life and our happy home. For a minute, I thought I needed to go back and fix things. I realized it was the enemy talking. I had to finally face the big question. *How could God bless a marriage that was established on a shaky foundation and built upon false pretenses?* I sought counsel from my mom and my aunt, both having dealt with abuse. The generational curse was illuminated and needed to be broken. The silence that continued for so many years was enough. I was going to be the one to break it.

After a much-needed break from everything, I finally returned home to San Diego and decided to take back control of my life. I knew it wasn't going to be easy because I was in for a fight when it came to Dylan being in our son's life. My parents, Preston and I were on the first flight back. What normally would be a comforting flight suddenly felt uneasy. Something wasn't right, or something wasn't going to go right. Once we landed, we headed straight to the courthouse and obtained a restraining order. That process felt like death. I was told there was nothing they could do because he was my husband. The most they could do was advise me to move out; but they also advised that he didn't have to leave because his name was also on the lease. It was a complete mess! I started to feel like my gaining control was already slipping away.

While sitting in the hallway waiting for the judge to call me back in, I silently prayed to God. "Please don't let this happen. Please don't let them tell me there's nothing they can do for me." As they called me back in, I remembered the ban that was placed on my husband. It prohibited him from any military property, including the military housing which we were living in. I hid this letter from the apartment office at the time because I felt like had I shown them the letter, my child and I would've been homeless, and I couldn't live with that. Starting to feel at ease, I knew that God was with me. I was called back into the courtroom where I explained to the judge that he was not allowed to be on military property due to his recent issues on base. The judge immediately issued a restraining order removing him immediately from the house. He couldn't be within five thousand feet of my son and me.

I knew serving him that order was not going to be easy, but it had to be done. Parking outside my house, that eerie feeling from before returned. Walking into my home, memories flooded me as I looked at the broken doors, the holes in the wall, the messy house. I realized my TV was missing. I wanted to break down, yet I knew I had to pull myself together and be strong enough to move on with my life. With the grace of God, me, my mom and my stepdad cleaned up the house. I went to the leasing office to ask if there was anything they could do to move me to a different place. Initially, they told me there was nothing they could do even with the restraining order. I had to go over their heads to protect me and my child. I went to the main office and the same woman who moved me the first time with open arms, arranged for me to move that same day.

I thank and praise God for what He's done for me. I could've been dead, could've lost my son, lost my clearance in the military; I could've lost everything because I was too afraid to be embarrassed by saying something. I had been too afraid to speak up, ask for help because I felt like I should've had my life together. I should have been able to control things in my life. The truth of the matter is, without God, we can't control anything. We are nothing without Him. When I look back and think about how far God's everlasting grace and mercy covered my son and I through this tumultuous time in our lives, I have no choice but to thank Him daily. God graced me with courage, strength and a village to help me leave my situation. My faith in God sustained me. Yes, I still struggle. But I trust the Lord each and every day to help me remain faithful to him. I trust that the fearless faith I had during my darkest moments will continue to help me navigate through the trenches and into my God-given purpose the remaining days of my life.

Psalms 91:14-16 says, "I will rescue those who love me; I will protect those who trust in my name. When they call me, I will answer; I will be with them in trouble; I will rescue and honor them. I will be worth them with a long life and give them my salvation."

I cling to this verse as part of my daily affirmations to keep me going even when I feel I'm at my lowest. It reminds me that God is always with me and will always protect me. Faith is a gift that each of us needs to accept. But so is Fearless Faith! God will give us everything we need to boldly live in His grace. Why is it that we often refuse His gifts? Why do we try to handle situations that are out of our control? I've learned Fearless Faith in God comes from discovering what is essential in life and being satisfied with it. It comes down to one simple thing, abiding in the presence of the Lord. When I began to seek to live and move and be in God's presence, I became Fearless!

Building Your Fearless Faith Muscle:

1. Pray without ceasing and always look to God first, not ourselves or others, for clarity.

2. Give up the belief that we are in control of our lives and pray for God's will to be done -not your own.

3. It is impossible to please God without Faith. Trust Him! Even though we can't see it, He is working behind the scenes to bring great things to pass in our lives.

4. Walk through your day with God.

5. Rest in the fact that God is for You!

Questions for the Reader

1. How do you show faith despite opposition?

2. How can your prayers reveal your faith?

3. Why does God treasure such servants as these women of *Fearless Faith*?

4. In what ways do you intend to imitate the lessons learned from *Fearless Faith*?

5. What does Fearless Faith mean to you?

About the Authors

MONICA FORTSON

Monica Fortson was born in Seattle, Washington. She grew up in the Kent School District and went on to attend Washington State University. Monica moved to Houston, Texas in 2005 and finished her degree at the University of Houston Downtown while working for Fortbend School District and then Houston Police Department.

Monica has been a Houston Police Officer for six years and is currently a detective in Child Sexual Abuse. During her time as an officer, she has worked with the Boys and Girls Club, Teen and Police Service Academy (T.A.P.S), and was the advisor for post 8300 for the Houston Police Explorers Program. She has worked as a DWI officer, Southeast night shift Patrol Officer, Community Service Youth Liaison Officer, and now a detective. Outside of work, she enjoys her horses and spending time with family and friends.

TATAYANDA JOHNSON-YOUNGER

Tatayanda Johnson-Younger is a highly motivated and talented Educator in the Dallas Independent School District. Her natural drive to reach and teach children from diverse backgrounds allows her to assist our future leaders to reach their highest levels of potential and growth in a competitive world.

Johnson-Younger is a dedicated and loving mother of three beautiful and gifted children: Serenity, Kevin Jr., and Charity. She enjoys writing poetry and performing Spoken Word. Johnson-Younger also finds joy in traveling and spending time with her family and friends.

She is a graduate of the University of North Texas in Denton, Texas where she earned a Bachelor of Arts degree in Psychology. Johnson-Younger also graduated from Concordia University Texas in Austin Texas with a Masters of Educational Administration degree. She was born in Dallas, Texas and resides in Lancaster, Texas. Johnson-Younger is a proud member of the amazing ladies of Delta Sigma Theta Sorority, Inc.

MICHELE JANEAU-MAJOR

Michele Janeau Major was born and raised in New Orleans, Louisiana. She prays that her testimony will reach others who are seeking and praying for God to show them the way to Him. She has learned that sometimes it is simple to let go and let God. The enemy plays tricks on us daily so we must walk by faith, stay strong and not by fear and doubt.

Her two strong parents taught her, her two brothers and sister the values of life and morals. They each passed along those same values to their children and grandchildren.

Michele's daily philosophy is to pray, keep a personal relationship with God and treat people the way she wants to be treated. To God be the glory!

DEBRA HUFF KELSO

I know what I'm doing. I have it all planned out--plans to take care of you, not abandon you, plans to give you the future you hope for."
Jeremiah 29:11 (MSG)

It seems God wrote these words especially for Debra Huff on that Saturday night in March when Priscilla Dean Price delivered her into this world. The late Marshall and Christine Huff later adopted her. Kelso was raised in a Christian home and has served in ministry since the age of six.

She accepted Christ as her personal Savior at the age of twelve. During her formative years, Kelso's love of the Lord was expressed through song as a member of the Children and Youth Choirs. She also served as organist for the Youth Choir. Kelso's parents planned for her to excel in music, but God had a different plan for her life.

She attended The University of Texas at Austin and majored in Social Work and relocated to the Dallas area in 1987. On Mother's Day, 1997, Debra united with St. John Church, Grand Prairie/Southlake, Texas, under the leadership of Pastor Denny D. Davis. The more Kelso tried to stay out of ministry; the more it seemed to 'get in' her. After four years of inactivity, she turned in her bench member card and began serving God through various areas of ministry.

Kelso serves effortlessly at St John. She is currently a member of the Pastoral Care Team. As a Facilitator in the Discipleship Ministry, she utilizes her spiritual gifts of Encouragement, Mercy and Discipleship to help lead others to victorious living through Christ. She has also been called to be an Intercessor.

In addition to serving at St. John, she is a staff writer for Epitome Magazine. Kelso has a passion to help those who are hurting and broken. She is very transparent and uses her testimony of God's grace and mercy in her life to encourage others through writing, speaking, preaching, teaching and mentoring others.

Kelso surrendered her will to God and accepted the call of ministry on her life in May 2005. In June 2009, her spiritual Father, Dr. Denny D. Davis, licensed her as a Minister of the Gospel.

November 2016, Kelso married her soulmate, David Kelso, and they live in Cedar Hill, Texas. Kelso is blessed to be the mother of one daughter, Arnelle Woods.

ANGELIQUE BROWN

Angelique Brown is a young adult who strives to be pure and to please God in all she does. She loves the Lord and knows she is nothing without Him. The challenges she's faced are not uncommon: a failed marriage and failed relationships, financial setbacks and other mentally and emotionally breaking moments all while trying to raise her daughter to best to her ability. Yet, she has gained an immeasurable strength through it all.

She is confident that all of it was part of God's plan to prepare her to be the woman of God she is today and to live in her God-given purpose. Angelique and her daughter live in Houston, Texas where they attend Lakewood Church under the leadership of Joel Osteen and John Gray. Her heart is set on helping other women know that with God there is a light at the end of the tunnel; with prayer, faith and action you can be healed when you trust Him with all your heart.

DR. MARCIA E. JACKSON

Dr. Marcia E. Jackson is a humble child of the Most High God. She accepted Jesus Christ as her Lord and Savior and was baptized at a very young age at the Mt. Corinth Baptist Church in her hometown of Shreveport, Louisiana. Shortly after graduating from Louisiana Tech University in 1994, she moved to the Washington, DC metropolitan area where she has resided for the last twenty-three years.

Dr. Jackson's passion is education. For the last nineteen years, she has enthusiastically supported students and families as a teacher, school counselor and administrator. She considers herself a leader, advocate and mentor in the field of education. She also enjoys helping to shape the next generation of educators as an adjunct professor with The George Washington University.

Dr. Jackson believes that Almighty God placed innate gifts, natural talents and sometimes hidden strengths in every person. She is anointed to draw out each person's personal gifts, uncover their latent talents and cultivate their amazing strengths. This is her life's work. She passionately believes that God has designed each of us to live our best life. Through the power of praying God's Word, she has witnessed situations and circumstances change. This has given her the fearless faith to pursue her Kingdom purpose while helping others along life's journey.

God has richly blessed Dr. Jackson to earn a Bachelor's degree in psychology from Louisiana Tech University, a Master's degree in school counseling from The George Washington University, a Master's degree in Educational Administration from Trinity University and a doctoral degree in Educational Administration and Policy Studies from The George Washington University.

She is the proud and doting mother of 19-year-old Richard, who is studying culinary arts to become a master chef with dreams of opening his own restaurant.

PATRICE ALEXANDER

Patrice Alexander is an amazing woman of God. Born and raised in Seattle, Washington, Patrice has a passion for bringing out the beauty in women. She is a licensed hair stylist and the owner of Creativ Conceptz specializing in healthy hair. Alexander's dedication to professionalism has changed the hair industry and inspired other stylists. One of the best hair cutters in Seattle, she is an artist who creates styles that have been admired by most everyone in the industry. With photos posted on various social media pages and websites, Alexander's desire is to elevate the hair profession to new heights of excellence.

Alexander is passionate about building relationships and is currently studying to be a licensed relationship coach. She is a faithful member of New Hope Missionary Baptist Church in Seattle. When she's not working, Patrice enjoys spending time with family and mentoring young girls. With her mission of inspiring others to live their best life, Alexander's desire is to empower young girls to believe that all things are possible and to never give up on their dreams.

EVELYN ALEXANDER

Evelyn Alexander is native of Seattle, Washington and has a love for volunteering and supporting others. Evelyn knows that GOD, FAMILY, and LOVE are the driving forces that bring her the most enjoyment in life, and she enjoys spending time traveling and learning.

Evelyn received her Bachelor of Arts Degree in General Business Administration at Seattle University, her Masters of Business Administration at City University, Masters Certification of Project Management from Stevens Institute of Technology, and is a certified Lean+ Value Stream Mapping and Accelerated Improvement Workshop Facilitator. Evelyn is also a certified Intercultural Development Inventory Administrator and Innovation and Inclusion Workshop Facilitator and most recently obtained her certification as a professional coach coaching employees, family, and friends to successfully reach their desired state of being.

Evelyn has been employed at the Boeing Company for over thirty years. In her many years at Boeing, she has served in numerous positions, on cross-functional teams, management, and business units.

She has served as the Co-Chair on the board of Northwest Black Pioneers Historically Black Colleges and University (HBCU) Tour touring HBCUs to coach and mentor local high school students on the benefits of post-high school education. Currently, she consults with the planning team for this organization.

Evelyn also serves as Co-Chair on the Diaconate board of New Hope Baptist Church where she is responsible for operations and administration and is a Deaconess supporting the church. She also is a member of the National Association of African Americans in Human Resources association.

Her business, *Essentially You!* Coaching services will be available mid-2018. For more information regarding Evelyn, contact her at:

Essentiallyyou2@gmail.com.

ALEXUS DOVER

Alexus Dover is a twenty-five-year-old native of Seattle, Washington. At the age of nine, her mother uprooted Alexus and her brother, Jeremy, and moved to Dallas, Texas. Upon graduating from high school, Alexus took an interest in the United States Navy. At the age of nineteen, with her parents' blessing, Alexus enlisted in the Navy to serve her country. In 2016, she was deployed to Bahrain for nearly eight months.

She is a nursing student at Texas Women's University in Denton, Texas. She is the proud mother of Preston Reid Dover, a vibrant three-year-old who keeps her on her feet.

Alexus is a member of Oak Cliff Bible Fellowship under the leadership of Pastor Tony Evans. She believes that sharing her testimony of how God delivered her from the cycle of abuse and the cycle of generational curses helped her to heal. Her relentless, unwavering, fearless faith is what made her the woman she is today.

Alexus is now ready to help other young women persevere through the trenches of heartache and pain by relying on God and breaking the chains of generation curses once and for all.

PRISCILLA HALEY
"VISIONARY"

Priscilla Haley is a Southern Girl born and raised in Shreveport, Louisiana. She is the President and Founder of "God Girlzs With A Vision," a foundation that is focused on introducing young girls to Jesus Christ and having a personal relationship with him through creative writing and vision boarding.

She is an Author, Speaker and Inspirational Writer with a desire to see women who have been broken, set from the bondage of their past. She is a Bestselling Author in "Soul Talk" an anthology of twenty women who share their soul-stirring stories of how they "let go and let God!"

Priscilla is a woman after God's own heart who unapologetically loves the Lord and has a heart for his people. A survivor of domestic violence and sexual abuse, her life story is one of courage and triumph. Her passion and life purpose is to help change the lives of women and confront the issues surrounding domestic violence.

Priscilla believes the emotional, mental and physical scars made her the confident and courageous woman of God she is today. Her life has been an open book to many as she finds joy in sharing, with much transparency, her struggles and testimony of being *broken*. She longs to be a voice of justice for all of the women who have lost their voice, or who are afraid to speak.

Priscilla is married to Darin Haley, and they are the parents of two children and five grandchildren. Priscilla and her husband are faithful members of Oak Cliff Bible Fellowship Church in Dallas under the leadership of Pastor Tony Evans. She is a mentor and volunteer for "Women Called Moses," an organization created to be an underground railroad for women of domestic violence. She also partners with "The Family Place," an organization that has been in the fight to stop domestic violence since 1978.

Priscilla's desire is help women navigate their way through the trenches, stand in their truth and understand God will take what has been broken and put it back together to be used for his Glory!

CPSIA information can be obtained
at www.ICGtesting.com
Printed in the USA
LVHW02s1519140418
573323LV00002B/2/P